Crisis Innovation

How Navy Bomb Disposal Technician's Think to Win

by

J. Keshig

ma, ms, msom, eds, dom, psyd

ACKNOWLEDGMENTS

I am indebted to the operational Bomb Disposal Technicians that volunteered to participate in this research. The Navy Bomb Disposal community's commitment to continuous improvement was demonstrated by the intensity of responses to the study and overall desire to help the next operator "on the X."

My mentor (with sons named Matthew and Mark), has always emphasized *humility* and *product*. I am eternally grateful for his guidance, uncommon ability to prioritize, and quiet patriotism.

Most importantly, I would like to dedicate this project to those that have lost their lives in the altruistic and ethically unambiguous field of bomb disposal. My hope is that this small endeavor might *"make it better"* in honor of their heroic sacrifice.

Bottom Line Up Front

Bomb disposal technicians are a peculiar lot. Navy Explosive Ordnance Disposal Technicians (NEOD) are the bomb disposal community subset that is most peculiar. NEOD are the most extensively trained bomb disposal technicians in the world with a selection and training pipeline that makes them the highest demand bomb techs across the globe. They parachute, dive, shoot, fight, drive fast, and deal with almost every type of crisis. Special Operations demand them as support personnel, but they are an eclectic bunch that maintains a command structure outside SOCOM. You will likely never see a leadership or good behavior book about them, as mundane tasks are not their specialty. However, they are the suspected to be the most innovative population of athletic nerds on the planet. When the effluent hits the affluent with an explosive, chemical, biological, or nuclear device, this byzantine and unusual group of individuals is who you want on your team.

This book is a result of my doctoral work studying NEOD from the perspective of innovation. Innovation drives the species through business and industry. Identifying and gaining access to the NEOD community is no small task, as insular does not begin to describe their way of being. Fortunately, I had a bit of experience in the NEOD world and was able to gain approvals for the study. Brace yourself for a walk on the wild side.

Scope of Study: The scope of this study consists of an academic literature review, qualitative interviews conducted with Navy Explosive Ordnance Disposal (NEOD) technicians (n = 22), and extensive analysis. The literature review presents foundational analysis of: (a) mindset, (b) motivation, (c) decision making, and (d) innovation across the general population and compares this information to the NEOD qualitative interview data. The primary focus was to obtain the essence of the NEOD lived experience, consolidate clusters of meaning, and increase knowledge about why NEOD voluntarily risk their lives against explosive devices (and plenty of other threats), how NEOD executes accurate decisions in a time limited environment, and how they innovate across a broad swath of advanced technologies in a crisis. The goal is knowledge transferability of innovation processes.

Findings and Conclusions: The data from this study is largely consistent with current research, but also offers a plethora of new insights about human performance. The NEOD mindset is multidimensional with three primary subsets: (a) motivation, (b) crisis innovation, and (c) decision-making. Within each subset, numerous components were identified. This study offers preliminary observations about the NEOD experience and how it might be transferred across the global EOD enterprise or perhaps, business and industry. NEOD is a community of aggressive altruists delivering life saving impact, a sort of last ditch line of defense.

Sad Reality: Regardless of strategies applied or technologies developed against terror, the problem will continue to escalate. The wonders of modern technology have a dark side; bad actors in the tiniest numbers now have access to tools and techniques for global disruption. The best counter to the problem is resilience and innovation in crisis. From your family, to small business, to large enterprises, the safest be

is to be a "resilient hard target" able to innovate in a crisis.

Notes:

1. While this study focuses on Navy EOD, it is important to remember that all EOD components possess amazing capabilities and traits in crisis innovation. My life has been saved by EOD technicians from the US Marine Corps, US Air Force, US Army, and Partner Nation EOD. For all my brothers and sisters in the EOD fight, a hat tip for going down range and *getting at it*.

2. Strict adherence to security protocols has been utilized throughout the text to protect the identities of the subjects, as well as ongoing operations. Many of the most dramatic operations will never become public knowledge in order to protect people, tactics, and procedures.

3. Vulgarity is included throughout this text, as it is a common lingua franca between trusted parties during informal military dialogue. The intent is to be authentic, not derogatory. In the larger scheme of life, words are merely noise, but use of explosive devices to kill innocents in the pursuit of an agenda is truly vulgar. We have lost track of what profane actually is....words ain't it.

4. All good ideas were gleaned from other bubbas, and all the errors would be mine alone.

5.   EOD technician's have had life experiences that often exceed the term "harrowing." The experiences included within this study are relatively tame, with the goal of meeting security requirements and protecting the technician from "friendly fire" of the administrative sort.

6.   I am using a pen name for this publication because I am not seeking fame nor fortune (beyond a harem of motorcycles). The goal is to highlight the NEOD role, advertise the good work they do, and help with transferability of concepts to business and industry.

7.   Yes, this study can be rather redundant based upon the academic requirements directed how it would be written. I felt it more important to push it out in an imperfect state quickly than spend time making a more marketable text.

8.   I do consulting supporting crisis innovation with a team of like minded people in order to solve intractable problems as well as selecting, building, and mentoring teams to win against all odds (doc@crisisinnovation.com). We only support democratic, rule of law folks seeking peace and stability.

TABLE OF CONTENTS

12

LIST OF FIGURES

CHAPTER ONE: OVERVIEW

Creativity is quaint, but without action and a mechanism for implementation, creativity doesn't amount to a hill of beans.

Innovation requires **action** to create value. From harnessing fire in ancient times to mapping the genome, hominids are an innovative group. As our species harnesses more complex technologies allowing much faster data processing (i.e. Moore's Law, et al), the acceleration of innovation for both good and evil also progresses unabated (Goodman, 2015; Thackray & Brock, 2015; Wittes & Blum, 2015). While horrific, the 9/11 attacks were also highly innovative, what some define as *malevolent innovation* (Cropley, 2010; Cropley & Cropley, 2015). If *necessity is the mother of invention* as Plato noted, crisis innovation is necessary in the current global Improvised Explosive Device (IED) fight because we are getting our asses kicked. Conservative estimates of global terror attacks demonstrated an approximate 80% increase in fatalities with more than 32,000 deaths in 2014 (LaFree, Dugan, & Miller, 2015). Violent Extremist Organizations can innovate on lengthier timelines, with the 9/11 attacks purportedly requiring more than 4 years of planning ("National Commission on Terrorist," A, 2004).

Explosive Ordnance Disposal (EOD) technicians respond to these attacks by leveraging advanced technologies, having severe time limitations to achieve results, and gambling their lives. While the business community utilizes the hyperbolic phrase *innovate or die*, the EOD technician as innovator literally risks becoming *pink mist* based upon the efficacy of their decisions. EOD technicians have more than skin in the game—their lives hang by the proverbial thread.

The most comprehensively trained EOD technicians in the world are from the United States Navy EOD force (NEOD). The training pipeline requires nearly 2 years to become an apprentice level responder for IEDs, underwater, chemical, biological, and nuclear ordnance, as well as obtaining diving, parachuting, and weapons qualifications. These robust qualifications are the *basic* career field entry requirement because NEOD has a methodical developmental process requiring several years to become a *senior* EOD technician, and from 5-10 years for the assiduously committed to qualify for the Master EOD ("Master Blaster") qualification. NEOD is a small physically robust force of less than 1600 highly qualified personnel, and most importantly, a constellation of *innovators* working on timed problems in any environment, with the highest human stakes. NEOD is virtually reminiscent of ninja, the traditional shadow warriors of Japan, because ninja are "meant to be different, more flexible and creative" (Man, 2013, p. 220).

Ultimately, this study is about the most powerful tool used in defeating explosive devices: human bomb disposal technicians. The bomb disposal specialty began in WWII and remains an *all volunteer* force noted for member's uniquely innovative and unusually courageous practices. Bomb disposal equipment improves as the threat evolves or new technology becomes available, yet tends to happen after the fact. As terrorists bring new devices to the fight, there may be no specific tool—the tool is the EOD technician creativity and skill. Bomb disposal technicians assess the situation, decide what tools are available to use and how to use them. Early research on bomb disposal technicians involved determining personality characteristics of successful British (n = 40) bomb disposal technicians (Cooper, 1982), as well as delving into learning characteristics of U.S. bomb disposal technicians (n = 100) (Bundy & Sims, 2007). While both studies provided exceptional insight into the EOD technician, the *paradigmatic* utilization of IEDs by terrorists has expanded the demand for increased knowledge about the EOD technician's themselves.

Violent Extremist Organizations (VEO's) use IEDs because *they work* (Moulton, 2009). VEO's leverage malevolent creativity and continually improve explosive devices. Responding to an improvised explosive item requires creativity and action. When combined, creativity and implementation equal innovation. Bomb disposal is high risk; indications are that, "flexibility and unconventionality in approaching each work event" are necessary (Cooper, 1982, p. 655). Finally, life and death decision-making is a key component of the EOD experience.

Background of the Problem

The essence of the NEOD technician's role can studied from the perspective of a *mindset*. A mindset is a mental disposition that mediates human responses to situational events (Asken, Christensen & Grossman, 2010; Dweck, 2006). NEOD technicians are altruistically motivated, innovate to solve problems, and execute high risk decision-making. Increased VEO IED events have increased the need for EOD technicians. EOD technicians are difficult to recruit and suffer significant attrition rates. Understanding the essence of the NEOD mindset defined as decision-making processes, innovation traits, and motivational factors will facilitate replicability.

Dweck (2006) identified two mindsets: fixed and growth. Fixed mindsets crave validation, while growth mindsets seek self-development (Dweck, 2006). The growth mindset builds on "the love of challenge, belief in effort, resilience in the face of setbacks, and greater creativity" (Dweck, 2006, p. 38). The malevolent creativity of IEDs require both growth mindset and resilience in order to respond.

Research in the field of applied psychology exists on the warrior mindset, with requisite emphasis placed upon mental toughness, resilience and self-assessment (Asken, Christensen, & Grossman, 2010). Ability to handle stress is a primary characteristic necessary for EOD technicians; experienced technicians demonstrated a muted physiological response to high threat situations when compared to new

EOD technicians (Cox, Hallam, O'Connor, & Rachman, 1983; O'Connor, Hallam, & Rachman, 1985). Defeating and explosive device requires being calm under pressure and the ability to self-assess. Zero Point, an industry leader in global EOD training and response offered the *performance under pressure mindset* of EOD into the international extreme sports arena by partnering with the Red Bull energy drink company (Lucio, 2015). The growth and warrior mindsets bisect with self knowledge. The Tao Te Ching was truly prescient when it stated, "He who overcomes others has force, He who overcomes himself is strong" (Laozi & Lau, 1963, p. 92).

Decision making processes. Academic perspectives on how the human decision-making process works is open to debate and fraught with the possibility that one size may not fit all. Kahneman (2011) identified two systems in the human decision-making process. System 1 is the emotional, intuitive and faster decision, while System 2 is logical, deliberate and slower process. Logical and deliberate decisions would seem to provide the most promising outcomes, particularly when time is not an issue. Options are weighed, alternatives considered, a series of calculations are performed and the result is the correct answer (Kahneman, 2011). Yet in EOD, there is often not enough time to function in an entirely methodical manner, because the problem set is of a brief, and entirely finite time period. Complex decisions that defeat explosive devices are both logical and rapid.

Gigerenzer's (2007) views diverged with Tversky and Kahneman (1982, 1983) on System 1 and System 2 theory, because Gigerenzer (2007) noted heuristics, or rules of thumb fulfilled a larger role in the process. Gigerenzer (2007) believed that a *fast and frugal* decision tree was used by experts to make decisions. Citing numerous cases of what laypeople might refer to as intuition, Gigerenzer (2007) identified a "search rule, stopping rule, and decision rule" (p. 152) method of processing data quickly and accurately. In the bomb disposal process, where multiple technologies might be used in new and innovative ways, heuristics could play a role.

Goleman's (2014) identification of *decision rules* blended facets of Tversky and Kahneman (1982, 1983) with Gigerenzer's (2007) views. Decision rules or rules of thumb, are simple terms used to discuss heuristics (Gigerenzer, 2007; Goleman, 2014). When discussing the need for emotional intelligence in leadership, Goleman (2014) used basic rules of thumb (i.e. the golden rule) on how to treat people as a baseline behavioral mechanism. More complex decisions relying upon System 2 type analysis are applied, as long as they do not clearly violate fundamental heuristics. Both Goleman (2014) and Gigerenzer (2007) inferred a decision-making process similar to an intellectual flow chart. This process parallels Chomsky's (1980) view of a universal grammar as the natural human ability to internalize and structure data.

In a larger sense, von Bertalanffy (1969), using general systems theory, proposed seeking out leverage points from interconnected problem sets. Whether using Kahneman's (2011) System 1-2 concept, or Gigerenzer's (2007) search, stop, decision rule, the EOD technician needs to filter a robust volume of data quickly, and then immediately move to resolve the crisis. Data processing time for the bomb disposal technician varies widely based upon the situation. Secondary or even tertiary devices may be emplaced in the same location as the initial IED, enemy forces could surge in their direction, or snipers could be targeting the EOD technician. Reducing *time on target* is a common EOD maxim because time spent at the device increases exposure to risk.

A bomb disposal scenario familiar to many EOD technicians is the identification of an anomaly (animal carcass, rock pile, fuel oil, crowd on a distant hill) along a commonly travelled route. The EOD technician processes environmental data quickly, determines the technology to respond, and performs complex mathematical calculations for explosive blast and fragmentation effects, because there may be a device in the animal carcass or along the road. The road indentation could indicate recent explosive device emplacement, the fuel oil puddle on the surface infers a potential mixture leak of explosive materials, and the folks on the hill could be spotters waiting to initiate a device. Military strategist and fighter pilot John Boyd (1976) referred to tactical quick reaction processes as the Observe, Orient, Decide, and Act Loop (OODA

Loop) (as cited in Ford, 2010). Speeding the OODA Loop through the use of appropriate data is a sustainable competitive advantage in many areas of life. Understanding the scaffolding of a possible NEOD OODA Loop within their mindset may be possible.

True experts possess faster OODA Loops in comparison to those with novice or intermediate skills (Ericsson, 2016; Gigenrenzer, 2007). Blind chess masters often defeat multiple opponents simultaneously with relative ease (Ericsson, 2016). Years of *deliberate practice* alter brain neuroplasticity thereby allowing faster pattern recognition and problem solving (Ericsson, 2016). Within the decision-making process, the level of expertise generating the decision improves outcomes. Based upon a review of training records, the average NEOD Master Technician possesses more than 8,000 hours of deliberate practice after progressing 5-7 years. Determining how the NEOD decision-making process functions in relation Kahneman's (2011) System 1 and 2 and Gigenrenzer's (2007) decision-making may yield sustainable competitive advantage across numerous industries.

Innovation traits. Innovation can be segmented into two categories: *disruptive* and *incremental*. Disruptive innovations are something entirely new and dramatic, the sudden paradigmatic event or technology that changes intellectual topography. In the world of terrorism, 9/11 was a defining disruptive innovation. Conversely, incremental innovation is less dramatic, but may outperform competitors over the long term (Anthony, 2008; Christensen, 1997; Naughton, 2012). Japanese entry into the U.S. automobile market is a case in point. Through continuous improvement (*kaizen*), Japanese manufacturers dominated the global automotive marketplace (Lyytinen, 2016). Winning in most corporate endeavors requires both disruptive and incremental innovation (Ritala & Hurmelinna-Laukkanen, 2012). Terrorists incrementally innovate and improve the efficacy of their attacks, with occasional disruptive technological innovations allowing sudden advantages (Dolnik, 2016). EOD Technicians incrementally improve their understanding of devices through forensic exploitation while also innovating to defeat new technologies through disruptive innovation. Incremental improvements are generally developed by the larger enterprise in EOD, at a nearly glacial pace. Conversely, disruptive innovations are the result of tactical EOD teams in a fight to "beat the device." "Putting your ass on the line" tends to release innovative capacity.

Innovative people possess five fundamental traits: (a) associational thinking, (b) questioning, (c) experimenting, (d) observing, and (e) networking (Dyer, Gregersen, & Christensen, 2011). Through careful observation and questioning, enhanced through networking, one may glean enough data to rapidly experiment (Dyer, Gregersen, & Christensen, 2011). All of this supporting data may yield insights to help with associational (or connectional) thinking. To *connect the dots* using associational thinking, one must first have the mindset and innovation behaviors to actually obtain the data (Dolnik, 2016; Dyer, Gregersen, & Christensen, 2011). When EOD arrives at a crisis incident, they need to *network* with people, assess a broad array of physical variables, perform risk mitigation, coordinate with numerous governmental entities, select the technologies to utilize, and utilize *associational thinking* to amalgamate the variables.

Similarly, exposure to the wider world through language, travel, and diverse activities can add to the potential innovators knowledge reservoir (Cotter, Pretz, & Kaufman, 2016; Dane, Baer, Pratt, & Oldham, 2011). Samli (2011) noted that *outside of the box thinking* is enhanced through flexible management boundaries.

Ericsson (2016) noted that real experts force themselves out of their comfort zones to improve. The current shift in the psychology of innovation towards a socio-cultural approach showed clear benefit in personal and group diversity (Sawyer, 2006). It's not just politically correct blather; mixed teams of diverse skills and backgrounds sharing a common goal tend to beat devices.

Innovation traits can also be impacted via organizational management style. Within the military world of counter-terrorism, an often repeated statement is that it "takes a network to beat a network" (McChrystal, Collins, Silverman, & Fussell, 2015, p. 84; Knoke, & Yang, 2008). An organism is a flat structure allowing for the free flow of ideas, networking, exposure, and associational connections (Brafman, & Beckstrom, 2006). Conversely, the military is hierarchy at its purest, and prone to the lethargic responses noted by Dixon (1976) in the *Psychology of Military Incompetence*. If flat organizations innovate more quickly through the five discovery skills inherent in their structure, it is unlikely they will be defeated by a hierarchical organization built upon vertical data flows (Brafman & Beckstrom, 2006; Meadows & Wright, 2008; McChrystal, 2013; McChrystal, Collins, Silverman, & Fussell, 2015).

NEOD personnel are frequently viewed by mainstream elements of the military as less rigid than the "regular" Navy. NEOD sailors use first names rather than rank during informal interactions, often have longer hair than mainstream peers, and generally seek to avoid highly structured events. NEOD may simply function as a flatter organization to respond in a more agile manner to global threats. Violating formal interaction protocols may enhance the opportunity to observe, question, and network because relaxed work environments have been shown to bolster innovation (Lewicka, 2010). Structural rigidity in the military is why terrorist innovation is so effective. Bad guys are not waiting for Higher Headquarters approvals of actions and have very few rules of engagement.

The flexibility to problem solve is impacted by the size, experiential level, interactive skills, and management of a team (Christensen, 2013; Beersma, Greer, Dalenberg, & De Dreu, 2016; Ullén, Hambrick, & Mosing, 2016). NEOD platoons are unusually small with eight personnel, but frequently divided into elements of two people with differing skill levels. Communication within teams, as well as management of teams may be non-standard. Team environmental and organizational structures correlate positively with innovation outcomes (Goleman, Boyatzis, & McKee, 2002; Sawyer, 2006; Wagstaff & Leach, 2015).

Motivation. While Maslow's (1970) hierarchy of needs places air, food, and water at the bottom of his pyramid structure, there may be a basement where survival in arduous circumstances resides. You probably won't need dinner if the IED you are working on *cooks off*. Motivation shapes behaviors by reducing response conflict and affecting working memory (Engelmann & Pessoa, 2014). Survival is normally the human prime directive, enhanced by purpose and meaning (Frankl, 1970). NEOD confronts mortality during most operations, and even in training venues. Perhaps motivational factors involved within NEOD operations move beyond basic survival mechanisms. Willingly challenging death may have both intrinsic and extrinsic motivational components. Numerous studies on creativity and innovation highlighted the importance of intrinsic motivation and optimism in creativity (Amabile, 1983; Amabile, Hill, Hennessey, & Tighe, 1994; Baas, De Dreu, & Nijstad, 2008). Purpose, mastery, and autonomy are the three pillars of motivation and support overall innovation in what Pink (2009) referred to as *motivation 2.0* (Forgeard & Mecklenburg, 2013).

Determining what motivates the NEOD technician, and how this might influence innovation within a crisis, is a key feature of the NEOD experience.

The Problem

Terrorists used more than 10,395 Improvised Explosive Devices (IEDs) from 2011-2014 (Overton, Craig, & Perkins, 2016). Failure to defeat the IED from 2011-2014 led to 70,196 casualties, with 54,752 being civilians (Action on Armed Violence, 2016). Explosive Ordnance Disposal (EOD) technicians respond to IEDs to protect personnel and property. Every IED event presents a series of unique challenges ranging from (a) the time allotted to defeat the device, (b) number of potential fatalities, and (c) environmental conditions. The primary tool of the EOD technician is a mindset consisting of innovation, motivation, and decision making skills. The EOD mindset allows for rapid and utilitarian innovation during explosive events where the stakes may include thousands of souls.

While extensive research exists regarding Counter-IED strategy and policy, very little is known about the primary weapon to defeat IEDs, the mindset of the EOD technician. The IED challenge is well understood, but knowledge regarding the human response mechanism to IEDs remains rudimentary. Hogan and Hogan (1989) completed a non-cognitive study on EOD students (n = 145) that shed light on what traits might help reduce EOD school attrition, but the subjects did not test under operational conditions. Understanding how EOD technicians function in crisis using their unique mindset could provide transferable knowledge to EOD training programs, other first responders, as well as the general public. Significant research demonstrated an ability to solicit expert cognitive experience, build training, and transfer this knowledge to new learners (Borders, Polander, Klein, & Wright, 2015). Global terror continues to expand, and the primary weapon of terror are IEDs, simply because IEDs are effective (Katagiri, 2014; Kaushik & Saha, 2016; Moulton, 2009). This study will help (a) to understand the mindset of EOD technicians, (b) codify the knowledge, and to (c) improve selection and training with the ultimate goal of saving more lives.

Significance

Between 2011 and 2014, IEDs produced more than 70,000 casualties (Action on Armed Violence, 2016). According to the

Global Terrorism Index, there have been more than 125,000 acts of terror since 1976 (Kluch & Vaux, 2016). EOD technicians respond to IEDs (Revill, 2016). Training and developing EOD technicians to respond to IEDs on a global scale is critical in maintaining peace and stability. While the global EOD force has vastly different equipment and procedures, the most important tool in development of an EOD technician is innovation, motivation, and solid decision skills under pressure. Bomb disposal technicians are *gutsy, courageous,* and even *heroic*, but under the veneer of public perception, they are "flexible, creative, and non-impulsive sensation seekers" (Cooper, 1982; Glicksohn & Bozna, 2000, p. 87). Understanding the NEOD mindset consisting of motivation, innovation traits and decision processes fulfills a knowledge gap about the best weapon to counter IEDs: the bomb disposal technician. Communities suddenly confronted with IED problems and beginning development of EOD programs may be able to leverage the knowledge of the EOD mindset to save lives.

Crisis innovation research within the NEOD industry has the possibility to impact innovation within other fields where the decision-making cycle is longer and the risks less catastrophic.

Learning how *to think like a bomb tech* in a high-risk crisis may be skill many people are interested in during the *forever war*.

Innovation in crisis, particularly of the high tech sort, will be a key component of future human resilience (Jerard & Mohamed- Nasir, 2015). Understanding the psychology of crisis innovation may be a component of a more resilient future. Regardless of technological and terror challenges, the greatest tool to protect personnel and property will remain the same: the ability to innovate quickly (Robb, 2007; Sciullo, Walklate, & Mythen, 2015).

Definitions and Key Terms

Navy Explosive Ordnance Disposal.

EOD Technicians are on call to respond to any type of ordnance, and they receive specialized training on how to handle chemical, biological, and even nuclear weapons. They investigate and demolish natural and man-made underwater obstructions, as well as prepare coastal regions for amphibious landings. EOD Technicians warn about potential threats–both in the United States and abroad. With expertise in the most conventional and unconventional explosives, they ensure the secure disposal of explosive weaponry. Whether getting the job done in a bomb suit or by utilizing state-of-the-art robotic technology, Navy EOD technicians are trained to use the most advanced tools of their kind in a role that's vital to the safety of servicemen and civilians. ("U.S. Navy Special Operations/EOD," 2016).

Basic EOD technician—*"slick bomb"*

The basic EOD technician is a graduate of the joint service EOD school and generally has less than 2 years of experience. These EOD technicians are learning the tools and processes of the EOD trade ("U.S. Navy Special Operations/EOD," 2016).

Senior EOD technician---*"Senior Tech"*

This terms refers to a Basic EOD technician that with full knowledge skills and abilities of the broad range of tools used by EOD after passing a lengthy qualification process ("U.S. Navy Special Operations/EOD," 2016).

Master EOD technician—*"Master Blaster"*

The master technician is the most experienced and qualified member of a Navy EOD team. Master Blasters develop young EOD technicians and ensure overall team safety. Not all NEOD members will become Master Blasters because of the intense qualification standards required. Master Blasters are most often in the Chief Petty Officer pay grades (E7-E9) (United States Navy Explosive Ordnance Disposal Association, 1992).

Limited Duty EOD Officer (EOD LDO).

This category refers to prior enlisted EOD technicians that became officers. Their role is to act as OIC of a team early in their career before moving on as EOD Readiness and Training Officers (RTOs). LDOs are the primary reservoir of tactical and equipment expertise.

Explosive Ordnance Disposal Officer—*"Coppertop"*

These individuals are EOD qualified commissioned officers holding at least a bachelor's degree and often a graduate degree. The EOD officers are the Officers in Charge (OICs) of units of action and progress on to senior strategic roles.

P1.

The EOD technician that makes the *long walk* to the hazardous item and conducts mitigation procedures on the explosive device.
P2.

The EOD technician directly supporting P1 at the incident site.

Render Safe Procedure (RSP).

When EOD conducts a procedure that will no longer allow the item to function as designed, it has been rendered safe.

Stop time.

A common EOD phrase used to denote a disabling of a device from progressing to detonation.

Organization

The goal of the following literature review demonstrates that

mindset is built upon scaffolding consisting of motivation,

innovation traits, and decision-making processes. The literature review includes research pertaining to common human experiences with rather significant gaps pertaining to more extreme endeavors. Extreme vocations requiring a mindset using rapid innovation, decision-making, and motivation may offer insight to increase efficacy in high stress experiences.

Chapter Three includes details of the research methodology of this qualitative study, as well as the goals and objectives. A data analysis will be included describing the results of the interviews with active duty Navy bomb disposal technicians. In this study, the topics to be discussed in Chapter Four are data from the problems presented in Chapter One. In Chapter Five, specific findings of the study are discussed.

CHAPTER TWO: BACKGROUND DATA

The term *mindset* is ephemeral, because the term can be attached to virtually any descriptor and the implications may change. Mindset is a general term to describe a way of thinking and the addition of an adjective merely produces a subset, or constellation of related concepts. Dweck (2006) developed an extensive body of research describing the key to success as a *growth mindset*. From child development to innovation within industry, Dweck (2015) defined growth mindset as more amenable to challenge, failure, and subsequent growth. Dweck (2006) is as a leader in the *psychology of success*. Many authors used the term mindset to outline a way of thinking or perhaps even an inclination towards specific goals. From the *Warrior Mindset* (Asken, Christensen, & Grossman, 2010), to the *Science and Technology Mindset* (Manitoba Network of Science and Technology, 1990), *Systems Mindset* (Carpenter, 2016), and *Global Mindset* (Den Decker, 2013), there appears to be no shortage of researchers using this term. The purpose of this study is to discuss the NEOD *mindset* including motivation, innovation, and decision-making skills. As Buddha noted in the ancient past, "what we think, we become" (Bukkyō Dendō Kyōkai, 1980, p. 9).

Determining what NEOD technician's think may expand knowledge of how they become effective.

The modern psychological concept of mindset reflects early social learning and cognition theory. These theories infer strong indications that nurture can sometimes overshadow nature in behavioral modeling and self efficacy (Bandura, 1985). Herzberger and Dweck (1978) conducted a study of 5th graders (n = 130) and found unsuccessful students focused on being wrong while successful students spent their energies trying to determine how to master the material. Rattan, Good, and Dweck (2012) examined the instructional style of four elementary school math students. Students comforted by teachers after poor performance assumed they were simply *not good at math*. Students encouraged to achieve math mastery changed their perspective to believe that learning new material required hard work (Rattan, Good, & Dweck, 2012). In an additional six studies, comforting praise by teachers for average results led to poorer student outcomes (Mueller & Dweck, 1998). In the case of these students, their mindset impacted actual outcomes (Mueller & Dweck, 1998; Good, Rattan, & Dweck, 2012). Gollwitzer (1986) noted similar tendencies of mindset to impact outcomes, especially in relation to taking action towards positive results.

The implications support the position that a *growth mindset,* which embraces challenges, because the *brain is a muscle* helps develop intrinsic motivation (Dweck, 2006, 2015). Conversely, a *fixed mindset* individuals suffer from a fear of failure and long term incompetence. With a fixed mindset, the assumption is a static capability regarding learning. Similarly, Duckworth and Peterson (2007) introduced the concept of *grit* that parallels with the growth mindset of Dweck (2006, 2016). Duckworth (2016) researched why some students tended to be more successful than others, regardless of innate talent or resources. Duckworth identified interest, practice, purpose, and hope as building blocks for grit. The growth mindset and grit concepts both indicate that *worldview largely determines outcomes.*

During WWII, Winston Churchill noted that EOD was a "task of the utmost peril," (as cited in Rachman, 2004, p.159) during an era when newly developed state sponsored ordnance items (bombs, mines, and rockets) regularly failed to function as designed. The EOD objective was to stop the device from detonating and determine how it worked through careful exploitation (Rachman, 2004). In the last two decades, the EOD challenge overwhelmingly consists of terrorist improvised devices that are constructed with malevolent creativity and often uniquely designed. Defeating hazardous items in the current era requires a specific, and likely unique, mindset. "Mindset impacts emotion, which alters biology, which increases performance" (Kotler, 2014, p. 15) in high risk sport. In the emotionally charged world of bomb disposal, mindset may function as a method to press on, no matter how dire the circumstances. When working on an IED, it is probably not a good time to think you cannot beat the device.

High risk mindset data is salient when considering Navy EOD technicians because no human is born an expert in High Altitude, Low Opening (HALO) parachuting, deep sea diving, shooting, and bomb disposal. These skills develop over many years of focused practice, requiring intense physical, emotional, and cognitive investments. The term *EOD Mindset* within the Navy Explosive Ordnance Disposal community describes a way of thinking that includes being motivated, innovative, and making good decisions. Good decisions in the NEOD lexicon include *protecting personnel and property*, not least of which is survival of the bomb disposal technician. There are a limited number of hominids that will run towards a bomb, and bomb disposal technicians have been described as "non-impulsive sensation seekers" (Glicksohn & Bozna, 2000, p. 87). Consequently, bomb disposal is an unnatural act, one driven by learned behaviors and perhaps a sense of altruism that appears to highlight the occasional power of nurture over nature.

The depth and breadth of skill sets an NEOD technician possesses are expansive, and technicians are sometimes referred to as a *multi-tool* or *Gerber* because of the diverse skill sets found in a single individual. NEOD responds to conventional ordnance (bombs, rockets, and sea mines), IEDs, chemical, biological, and nuclear weapons. NEOD frequently supports Special Operations Forces (SOF), Federal and local law enforcement, and a plethora of partner nations. NEOD also delivers a robust volume of Humanitarian Mine Action support helping train partner nations in the disposal of retrograde ordnance (landmines and stockpiles of leftover bombs). NEOD travels to work by any method needed; parachute, small boat, underwater, or rappelling from a helicopter. NEOD shoot weapons expertly, excel in unarmed combat, and attend professional driver courses. Many are trained in foreign languages, use advanced robotics, rapidly conduct advanced mathematical calculations, and communicate on highly complex networks. NEOD works in small teams of 2-8 people to solve intractable high risk problems without fanfare.

This study defines the NEOD mindset as: the motivation to improve outcomes, protect personnel and property; innovation through combination, leverage or adoption of diverse technologies or human networks; near real time decision making in high stakes environments; with the goal of defeating explosive, chemical, biological, and nuclear hazards on land or underwater. NEOD activities are both outcome and process focused (outcome is of vastly greater importance than process).

Motivation

Gollwitzer (1999) noted motivation is a "primary cause of behavior" (cited in Smelser & Baltes, 2001, p.10109). The driving force in motivation is multidimensional, with four components believed to produce behavior: genetic, learning, sociality, and cognition (Petri & Govern, 2013). The prime directive as animals is to continue the species, and although this might seem basic, the manner in which learning, sociality and cognition complicate the process are a challenge to the species (Buss, 2015). Further physiological perspectives on motivation include instinct (Epstein, 1982), homeostasis (Nolte, 2007; Stagner, 1977) and arousal mechanisms (Malmo, 1959). While the common justification for physiological arguments are that humans eat when they feel hunger, this does not appear to answer all conditions. Some people eat to the point of corpulence, while anorexics barely eat at all. Gender definition issues remain fascinating as well (Buss, 2015). If the species is pre-programmed to reproduce, determining the genetic directive in the asexual population becomes a significant exception (Buss & Schmitt, 1993). Clearly, genetic, instinct, and arousal are factors in motivation, but not completely definitive. NEOD performs tasks that dramatically increase risk of death and may be indicative of unique motivation.

The development of learning and motivation theory provides additional insight to human motive (Bandura, 1977; Spence, 1956; Hull, 1943). Through learning, humans can develop complex motives that fuel behavioral decisions. Reward and punishment often motivate people towards behaviors that include positive outcomes (Bandura & Schunk, 1981; Rolls, 2007). Motivation

cognition impacts learning because learning is dependent upon social

context, culture, individual world view and level of control (Amabile,

Hill, Hennessey, & Tighe, 1994; Amabile, 1994; Pittman, 1987).

While learning and cognition have a role within motivation, there

appears to be cases where this strategy remains insufficient. An

exception to learning and motivation theory was Draper Kaufman,

the founder of NEOD and Navy SEALs. Mr. Kaufman was initially

denied entry into the U.S. Navy during WWII because of his inferior

eyesight. Kaufman simply joined the British military and became a

Bomb Disposal Technician with minimal concern for rewards or the

status quo of the Navy (Bush, 2004). Kaufman appeared outside

cultural norms with limited genetic predisposition for NEOD.

Maslow (1943,1970) originally studied successful people to

determine what motivated them to achieve more than their peers.

Maslow ultimately formulated a hierarchy of needs that led to an

understanding of the human desire to achieve self actualization.

Maslow's theory of self actualization was updated to include "(a)

evolutionary function, (b) developmental sequencing, and (c) their

cognitive priority as triggered by proximate inputs"

(Kenrick, Griskevicius, Neuberg, & Schaller, 2010, p. 293).

Cognitive priority and evolutionary function may provide insight to

NEOD motivation. The positive psychology movement studies

robust human performers to yield knowledge about how to improve

the human condition (Seligman & Csikszentmihalyi, 2000). A

closely related concept from the positive psychology movement has

been the idea of an optimal state called *flow*. Flow is the feeling of

joy and timelessness that happens when we engage in an activity of

deep meaning (Wilder, Csikszentmihalyi, & Csikszentmihalyi, 1989).

NEOD technicians may experience a feeling of flow when

performing risky tasks that fuels motivation.

Motivation and High Risk Activities: The Knowledge Gap

Lengthy and robust research exists regarding motivation

within normative populations. A *Google Scholar* search conducted

in September, 2016 found 403,000 research articles or books on

student motivation, 372,000 on business motivation, and 175,000

pertaining to medical practitioner motivation. Studies regarding

NEOD personnel and why they enter, and ultimately remain in the

occupation are extremely limited, with Cooper's (1982) study of

successful bomb disposal personality characteristics calling for further research. Bundy and Sims (2007) sought skill commonalities within military EOD students, and also noted the need for further research. Zero results in *Google Scholar* were achieved in a September 2016 search for NEOD mindset, innovation, motivation, and decision-making. Since 2005, research into human performance psychology of extreme sport players may provide insight. Extreme sports include high risk physical activities such as BASE jumping, high altitude skiing, massive wave surfing, extreme rock climbing, and waterfall kayaking (Brymer & Schweitzer, 2013). In several studies, extreme sport players are described as thrill seekers, or type T personalities, committed to thrill and sensation seeking (Monasterio, 2013; Self, Henry, Findley, & Reilly, 2007). Brymer and Schweitzer (2013) identified six motivational factors for extreme sports practitioners: Results (a) freedom from constraints, (b) freedom as movement, (c) freedom as letting go of the need for control, (d) freedom as the release of fear, (d) freedom as being at one, and (e) freedom as choice and responsibility (p. 27). Extreme physical activities within the NEOD occupational skill set are similar to extreme sports (mountain climbing, diving, skydiving, and high speed driving). While NEOD is clearly altruistically oriented, extreme sport does provide the general public with entertainment. Understanding why the NEOD operator fulfills this role is of academic interest.

Another facet of motivation pertains to the often cited triad of purpose, autonomy, and mastery as the key pillars (Gillard, Gillard, & Pratt, 2015; Pink, 2009). Fragoso, Holcombe, McCluney, Fisher, McGonagle, & Friebe (2016) conducted a study on 102 Emergency Management Service (EMS) first responders and found that purpose was the most significant motivator. EMS responders are a high stress industry with some basic parallels to the NEOD force. Sudden responses, diverse technologies, and rapid decision-making are all functions of the EMS responder (David-Persse, 2015). The primary difference between EMS and NEOD is that NEOD risk is much broader because both the first responder and significant portions of the local population may die during the response. EMS responders save lives, usually one healthcare crisis at a time, with occasional disaster responses where patients are treated serially. Determining how NEOD defines purpose in the course of this study may be important, particularly because the demand for NEOD personnel will continue to increase (Bundy & Sims, 2007).

NEOD operators likely experience the optimal feeling of *flow* in the course of disarming a bomb, parachuting, diving, or conducting other high risk and complex activities (Csikszentmihalyi, 1990). Years of deliberate practice in an athletic and technological endeavor being used in a wickedly charged environment must provide significant stimulus (Ericsson, 2016). Since "high risk activity can profoundly alter consciousness and significantly enhance mental abilities," (Kotler, 2015, p. 13), the NEOD operator is likely in a heightened psychological state during high risk activities. Hardie-Bick and Bonner (2015) conducted an ethnographic study of rock climbers and skydivers that found a high degree of *flow* in participants. *Flow* may act as a motivational component for experienced NEOD operators, thereby supporting both ascension and retention in the NEOD community. *Flow* as a motivator could be a subset of the NEOD mindset and directly relates to this research project.

Gaining insight on how genetic, learning, sociality, and cognition components of motivation influence the NEOD operator will be pursued via self reporting in this study. Determining factors of how operators are over-riding the survival mechanism is a conundrum.

Fehr and Fischbacher (2003) noted that altruistic personalities were able to sway groups, even egoist groups, towards altruistic behaviors. Perhaps an NEOD subset of motivation includes altruistic beliefs that are reinforced by the group mindset. Kotler (2014) notes that the "most primary of primary drives" (p. 15) is to avoid death. Choosing to enter a high risk occupation where death is common appears to be counter intuitive.

Innovation

In the general sense, innovation "consists of a new combination of existing ideas, capabilities, skills, and resources" (Sawyer, 2013, p. 7) combined to achieve an outcome. Innovation is a major focus of industry (Suckley, 2015). Innovation is so important that governments actively pursue policies with hopes of achieving competitive economic advantage (Bhat, 2015). "Innovation is an explanatory factor in performance between firms, regions and countries" (Sawyer, 2013, p. 13; Sawyer & Bunderson, 2013). Bomb disposal technicians acting in innovative ways to defeat explosive hazards provide a stabilization advantage to their country. Governments, by design, seek stability, growth, and sometimes control (Fitzpatrick, 2003). Mitigating terror incidents and reducing loss of life are therefore national and international objectives. The most popular weapon of terror is the IED and EOD technicians are the primary response mechanism (Moulton, 2009). Understanding the human component of response is supported by this study.

Innovation is an area of intense academic research, yet not well defined. Crossan & Apaydin, (2009) conducted a metadata analysis of 525 peer reviewed journal articles concerning innovation. The publication period covered 27 years of frequently cited innovation studies. Crosson and Apaydin (2009) noted that "no consistent definition of innovation could be found, nor was any dominant pattern of what type of innovation practices would lead to consistently beneficial outcomes identified" (p. 1164). Lopes, Kissimoto, Salerno, Carvalho, and Laurindo (2016) conducted a biblio-metric analysis of 36 years (1975-2011) study of innovation research articles (82) and found innovation to be multidimensional with weak definitions. Each study indicated a need to consider industry specific subsets of innovation, as well as the outcomes desired by those entities (Fagerberg, Mowery, & Nelson, 2005). This study supports understanding the specific innovation subset of NEOD crisis response.

An innovation focused educational literature review by Pisanu and Menapace, (2014) found four key features of managing innovation: (a) organizational structures, (b) individual characteristics, (c) training methods, and (d) training content. In a careful look at eastern UK industry, Neely and Hii (2014) found organizational culture culture, resources, competences, and networks to be the defining features of innovation. Jalonen (2011) in an innovation review of 101 journal articles found uncertainty to be a major feature of the innovation milieu. Considering the broad factors affecting innovation, reverse engineering our understanding from the ground level upwards is beneficial. *Lead users* are far more innovative than scientific or management researchers (Fagerberg, Mowery, & Nelson, 2005; von Hippel, 2013). Schumpter (1911), the veritable godfather of innovation research, identified qualitative research as the best method of understanding innovation. By using qualitative research at the lead user level of bomb disposal, one may expect to understand the innovation process more completely, supporting the need for this study.

Crisis Innovation from the Ground Up

This study focuses on crisis innovation at the tactical level, across diverse technologies, in a time restricted and high risk environment. Because limited research exists on this specific population or problem set, there may be parallels in relation to standard innovation practices to clearly differentiate the type of innovation considered in this study (*crisis innovation*):

Crisis innovation in this study is defined as: a combination, leverage or adoption of diverse technologies, data or human networks with the goal of defeating explosive, chemical, biological, and nuclear hazards on land or underwater. It takes place in a severely time restricted environment with risk of death to the operator and nearby population. It is outcome focused.

Individual innovators have been studied exhaustively. Buel (1960) identified 18 creativity and innovation traits of individuals within the oil industry as assessed by their managers. Amabile (1983) extended the knowledge of innovation traits by considering the social interaction capabilities of innovators. Innovators actively question, observe, experiment, and network, all of which benefit from social interaction skills (Dyer, Gregersen, & Christensen, 2011). A broad base of experience or exposure to other cultures adds an additional dimension, as well as *platform skills* or what might best be referred to as a basic understanding of the equipment one hopes to leverage (Brusoni & Prencipe, 2009; Cotter, Pretz, & Kaufman, 2016; Costa-Font, Courbage, & Mina, 2009; Sawyer 2013). The innovator requires enough knowledge of the things combined to understand what rules might be manipulated to achieve advantage (Cropley, 2011). Determining what innovation traits from business and industry parallel traits within the NEOD community may be determined by this study.

Tying the aforementioned personal traits together to innovate demands associational thinking (Dyer, Gregersen & Christensen, 2011), or what Cropley (2006) referred to as *divergent thinking*. Few humans would connect the experience of removing nettles from their pants after wandering in the mountains with the concept of manufacturing Velcro, but that is exactly what the chemist Georges de Mestral achieved (Budde, 1995). However, a paradox exists in innovation thinking (Cropley & Cropley, 2008). While blending divergent thoughts, the innovator also needs to be able to think congruently enough to evaluate the innovation being considered (Cropley, 2011, 2006). The outcome provides insight into why heterogeneous groups outperform homogenous groups in innovation tasks (Basadur & Basadur, 2011) and is important to this study to determine if this parallels NEOD thinking.

The time from innovation to execution can depend upon the individual, the industry, and linkages (Fowinkel, 2014; Gaubinger, Rabl, Swan, & Werani, 2014). The previously mentioned innovation studies all have a specific research gap relating to timeline. Simply stated, corporate research innovation is measured in timelines lasting months, weeks, and years. Cropley and Cropley (2015) began this topic in their discussion of the 4 Ps of innovation: (a) person, (b) product, (c) process, and (d) press. *Press,* used by Cropley and Cropley (2015) and Cropley (2015, 2010), is the social context and pressure that engenders innovation. Within NEOD, press could be considered the forced time window and social pressure to defeat an explosive device. In the world of bomb disposal, a broad range of categories exist requiring differing levels of urgency to innovate. Devices found in remote and uninhabited locations are not of the same urgency involving larger devices in highly populated areas. Plattner & Leukert (2015) argued the innovation timeline is a problem framing issue, but by re-thinking the problem set, innovators can adjust timelines to improve outcomes.

Decision-Making

How humans categorize information to make decisions depends upon the problem, the amount of time available, and the risk involved. Tversky and Kahneman, (1983, 1975, 1974, 1973, 1972) long argued that human decision-making is divided into System 1 (emotional, intuitive) and System 2 (deliberate, logical) processes (Kahneman, 2011). Kahneman and Tversky (1979) followed to develop prospect theory, the demonstration that people use heuristics to determine losses and gains and then make a decision based upon their risk appetite. A key feature of prospect theory is that each individual's use of anchoring is a cognitive benchmark (Kahneman & Tversky, 1979). Anchoring is over-reliance upon initial data (Kahneman & Tversky, 1979). A typical example is the often inflated price on a new car. Once negotiations begin at the inflated price, increases or decreases within a self defined price range more amenable to a consumer (Kahneman, Slovic, & Tversky, 1982). Kahneman (1979, 1975) ultimately won the 2002 Nobel prize in economics based upon this work in decision-making. Time restraints and high risk were not primary factors in considering decision theory by Kahneman, Slovic, or Tversky (2011, 1982, 1979,

1975, 1974, 1972). Understanding the essence of crisis innovation within NEOD justifies this study because both high risk and time constraints are included.

Gigerenzer's (2007) view of decision-making diverged from that of Tversky and Kahneman (1982, 1983, 1972,1974, 1975) on System 1 and System 2 theory. Gigenrenzer (2014, 2004, 2003, 2002, 1999) believed heuristics, or rules of thumb fulfilled a much more powerful role in decision-making, without a loss in outcome efficacy. Gigerenzer (2007) argued that a "*fast and frugal* decision tree" (p. 179) was used by experts to make decisions. Using a "search rule, stopping rule, and decision rule" (Gigenrenzer, 2007, p. 152) method of processing data quickly and accurately, humans can calculate extremely rapid and positive outcomes without performing System 2 calculations. While Gigenrenzer and Gray (2011) delved into time and risk decision through research in emergency medicine and confirmed highly trained physicians use heuristics in decision making, Kumar (2015) validated this concept within the British hospital network, where physicians used quick rules of thumb in decision-making. Identifying if NEOD utilizes *fast and frugal* decisions in crisis innovation supports the utility of this study.

The concept that decision rules drive much of human decision-making is increasingly popular. From using decision rules as a business leadership tool to artificial intelligence development, fast and frugal appears to provide good outcomes quickly (Goleman, 2013; Nunes, Miles, Luck, Barbosa, & Lucena, 2015). This process parallels Chomsky's (1980) view of a universal grammar as the natural human ability to internalize and structure data, or general systems theory view of leverage points (von Bertalanffy, 1969). Government and industry benefitted from computer modeling for fast and frugal decisions. Cui (2015) helped model ideal decisions for the Spanish government agencies that would allow them to compare their own decisions to those of a fast and frugal model. Conceptually, fast and frugal heuristics work in most cases, yet lack the data to determine if they work when the stakes are incredibly high. Determining if NEOD uses heuristics may advance knowledge of the decision-making field.

Decision Making and Crisis

Management of crisis is a critical skill to increase human resilience to both terrorism and natural disasters. Naturalistic Decision-Making (NDM) theory developed in 1989 and combines many facets of Gigenrenzer (2007) and Kahneman's (2011, 1982) work, but adds stress, situational awareness, and training (Huder, 2012; Klein, 2015). NDM builds on the Recognition-Primed Decision-making model (RPD) and requires subject matter expertise (Lintern, 2010). Rather than cognitively scrolling in System 2, or relying on heuristics, NDM uses situational awareness and expertise to make the right choice immediately (Huder, 2012; Klein, 2015). These sorts of quick reaction processes identified by John Boyd were initially used by fighter pilots. Boyd (cited in Ford, 2010) termed this process the Observe, Orient, Decide, and Act Loop (OODA Loop). NDM is a sophisticated of the OODA loop concept that allows personnel to execute sound decisions (Lipshitz, Klein, Orasanu, & Salas, 2001). Exploring how NEOD decision-making in crisis in relation to NDM and RPD support the need for this study.

Extensive training and years, if not decades of experience, can result in better decisions. Experienced firefighters use their intuition to leave buildings immediately before a collapse (Klein, 2008). Blind chess masters can play scores of simultaneous games and win (Ericsson, 2016). Clearly, decision-making skills are benefitted by both the experience of the host, the decision making process utilized, and the level of risk.

McCullar (2013) documented the importance of visualization of potential outcomes to responses in crisis. Envisioning past events based upon experience and future outcomes based upon technical knowledge can help in crisis decision-making. McCullar's (2013) model emphasized the ability to learn from the study of past events, as well as the importance of carefully reviewing of decisions after a crisis. Post event incident review appears to help build decision architecture or a mental model for the individual (Hudar, 2012; Lintern 2010). Decision-making architecture can be culturally dependent (Bernhardsdóttir, 2015). Decisions requiring group input add further complexity (Dowell, 2016). NEOD works in multi-cultural teams with divergent levels of expertise and broad experience.

Conceptual Framework

This goal of this study is to understand the NEOD mindset as seen through the lens of motivation, innovation, and decision-making skills. Through use of qualitative research based upon self-reporting of active duty NEOD technicians, increased knowledge of how NEOD technicians think, what motivates them, and most importantly how they make decisions to innovate, may expand knowledge of crisis innovation. The global crisis in terrorism created increased challenges from malevolent creativity (Cropley, 2010). Cooper's (1982) study of successful bomb disposal technicians (n = 20) demonstrated a propensity for creativity, unconventional thinking, and flexibility. Understanding how successful NEOD operator's mindset functions may be replicable globally and provide irreplaceable data on how one can build better bomb disposal technicians globally.

Dweck (2015, 2006) demonstrated the positive impact of a growth mindset in improving performance. People who enjoy solving complex problems and can accept constructive feedback fare better in life (Dweck, 2006). From a positive psychology standpoint, identifying and understanding exemplars of performance to learn why they succeed can be useful knowledge to others seeking to excel (Seligman & Csikszentmihalyi, 2000). NEOD technicians are similar high performance athletes with advanced technical skills and fulfill a critical societal role (U.S. Navy, 2016). The way NEOD views the world through mindset with a focus on their self reported belief system may provide insight to quickly develop more EOD technicians of greater proficiency and therefore supports the focus of this study.

Motivation, as a subset of mindset in this study, may fulfill the need to understand why NEOD personnel volunteer to perform this dangerous mission. Whether motivation is evolutionarily advantageous as Buss (2015) argued, or based upon the multi-dimensional perspective of genetic, learning, sociality, and cognition, one does not know (Petri & Govern, 2013). Perhaps purpose (Gillard, Gillard, & Pratt, 2015; Pink, 2009) and / or flow (Wilder, Csikszentmihalyi, & Csikszentmihalyi, 1989) are the driving forces in motivation. Because NEOD is dangerous, an all volunteer force (U.S. Navy, 2016), and the training is arduous (Hogan & Hogan, 1989), NEOD possesses significant motivation.

Business people discuss innovation and economic death. NEOD lives innovation and sometimes experiences actual death. To understand innovation in crisis, one needs to understand how NEOD succeeds in the field. Violent Extremist Organizations (VEOs) are creative, and defeating malevolent creativity requires innovation (Cropley, 2015, 2010). Dyer, Gregersen, and Christensen (2011) determined that innovators actively question, observe, experiment, network, and connect differing data points using associational thinking. Understanding how NEOD may use questioning, observing, experimenting, networking and connectional thinking may provide insights into crisis innovation. Additionally, Pisanu and Menapace (2014) noted four key features of managing innovation: (a) organizational structures, (b) individual characteristics, (c) training methods, and (d) training content. NEOD innovation may be impacted by their organizational structure, personal characteristics and training thereby demonstrating a need for this study. Limited understanding of innovating in abbreviated high risk timelines demonstrates a clear knowledge gap. Determining what insights field NEOD operators might share in regards to innovation at the ground level may increase our understanding of crisis innovation.

Relevant decision-making research falls into three categories: System 1 & 2, heuristics, and Naturalistic Decision-Making (NDM). Tversky and Kahneman (1983, 1975, 1974, 1973, 1972) championed the idea that one formulates fast emotional decisions via System 1, or deliberate logical decisions via System 2. By contrast, Gigenrenzer (2014, 2004, 2003, 2002, 1999) relied on heuristics and one's supposed natural propensity to decide using fast and frugal decision trees. NDM relies on a large body of Gigenrenzer's (2014, 2003) work, but emphasizes the utility of specialty expertise in building the heuristic architecture. Of the three perspectives on decision-making, only NDM focuses on crisis response (Lintern, 2010). Qualitative research on NEOD may help determine what successful crisis decision-making looks like from the tactical level.

Summary

Understanding how to innovatively respond to the threat of malevolent creativity may benefit by studying individuals who respond successfully. NEOD is a community that responds to unique problems in time controlled, high risk environments. Their unique mindset comprised of motivation, innovation, and decision-making skills is a rich resource for investigation, because of the potential to expand current knowledge of how NEOD thinks to win through motivation, innovation, and decision-making. Increased understanding from self-reporting of tactical level operators may expand knowledge of why they do this task, how they innovate in a crisis, and what heuristics (if any) drive their decision-making. Chapter Three includes details of the research methodology of this qualitative study, as well as the goals and objectives. A data analysis will be included describing the results of the interviews with active duty Navy bomb disposal technicians

CHAPTER THREE: METHODOLOGY

The purpose of this phenomenological study is to explore the NEOD technician's experience responding to crisis situations using innovation, motivation, and decision-making skills. Available research on bomb disposal technician's is limited (Bundy & Sims, 2007; Cooper, 1982; Hogan & Hogan, 1984). The NEOD experience was explored from the operational level where high risk activities take place. A qualitative phenomenological was the most advantageous method to capture the essence of the NEOD experience. This chapter includes description of the study's ontological, epistemological, and philosophical components.

Research Method

The purpose of this phenomenological study is to explore how NEOD understands and experiences the NEOD mindset through the triad of crisis innovation, motivation, and decision-making. There were 6,320 IED attacks between 2011 and 2015 with 105,071 people reported killed or injured (Action on Armed Violence, 2016, May 27) yet no current literature exists on the primary counter to IEDs, the EOD mindset. The literature gap is problematic, because the EOD technician's choices will always be the most powerful weapon to defeat a device (Bundy & Sims, 2007; Draper, 2006; Gurney, 1993, Laska, 2015; Revill, 2016). Technologies, geographic locations, and terror devices change continually, often through malevolent creativity (Cropley, 2015). The forward deployed and highly engaged NEOD technician was the voice of this qualitative investigation, because that person conducts the actual emergency response. Understanding direct knowledge from a phenomenological perspective informs and motivates questions, intentionality, and conclusions (Benetka & Joerchel, 2015; Creswell, 2013; Smith, Flowers, & Larkin, 2009; Wiggins & Schwartz, 2015).

Through a phenomenological based qualitative study, the primary research questions are as follows (see Figure 1):

- To what extent do NEOD technicians innovate with new techniques during a crisis?

- To what extent do NEOD technicians use *rules of thumb* when responding to a crisis?

- What motivates NEOD technicians to perform their exceptionally dangerous role?

Exploring these questions at the operational level based upon the ontological, epistemological, and philosophical scaffolding outlined in this segment may yield meaningful results (Creswell, 2007).

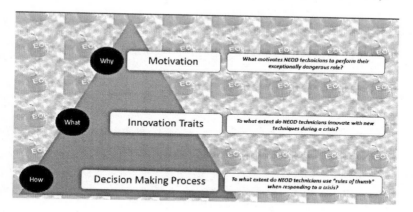

Figure 1: Illustration of the crisis innovation and the Navy EOD mindset.

Ontology, Epistemology, and Philosophical Scaffolding

How this study regards knowledge ontologically, arrives there epistemologically, as well as the methodology used to study knowledge are important facets of this research. NEOD technicians likely view reality differently than the general population, and even among themselves (Maul, 2013). Understanding self-reported realities offers this study a depth and breadth of experiential data as defined by actual participants. Interviewing NEOD tactical operators about what, how, and why they they defeat explosive threats offers rare insight to a unique problem set (Moustakas, 1994).

Understanding and exploring the NEOD mindset requires accessing motivated personnel, that make decisions and innovate in crisis because knowledge results from "the subjective experiences of people" (Creswell, 2013, p. 79). Epistemology includes the focus with human judgment and reasoning and thereby a key component of the NEOD mindset (Bishop & Trout, 2005). Using a qualitative approach best serves exploration of how and what NEOD technicians experience because data is garnered at the point closest to where NEOD activities take place. In this study, a forward deployed NEOD unit embedded in Asia provides a robust venue. The study will use a constructivist approach to discover and describe participant perspectives of the world they experience (McWilliams, 2015).

Huta (2016) noted that meaning is a subjective experience; to understand a subjective experience, knowledge is gained from self-reporting of participants in an open ended dialog. Conducting the study open mindedly may help in understanding multiple realities (Polkinghorne, 1989). The goal of this research is to explore and understand how NEOD technicians understand innovation, utilize heuristics, and motivate themselves to defeat explosive devices in crisis.

Qualitative Phenomenology

A phenomenological qualitative methodology was used in this research. Phenomenological qualitative research met the needs of this study because understanding the subjective and cognitive experience of NEOD allowed participants to describe their experiences (Giorgi, 1997; Giorgi, 1992; Smith, Flowers, & Larkin, 2009; Smith, 2011A, 2011B). The qualitative approach to psychological work is decidedly realist, focusing on meaning as defined by the participants (Michell, 2004). This method of inquiry includes selection to understand the meaning of the NEOD mindset as a *notable phenomenon* (Creswell, 2013). Capturing the reality of the NEOD mindset phenomenon is the goal (Finlay, 2014). The phenomenological approach is widely used in sociology, medicine, and psychology (Bogdan & Taylor, 1975; Creswell, 2013; Moustakas, 1994; Smith, Flowers, & Larkin, 2009).

Edmund Husserl (1859-1938) was a German philosopher who popularized phenomenological investigation with the goal of understanding complex meaning from direct experience (Merriam, 2002). Capturing direct experience supports this NEOD study by capturing lived experiences of participants to determine general meanings of the NEOD mindset with a focus on innovation, decision-making, and motivation (Creswell, 2013; Sousa, 2014). The goal of this study is to "understand these common experiences in order to develop practices or policies" (Creswell, 2013, p. 81) to train bomb disposal technicians globally, as well as develop policies advantageous to crisis innovation skill transference, built upon *ground truth* from operators.

Using a phenomenological approach, this study relies upon processes articulated by Creswell (2013) and largely built upon the research of Moustakas (1994). The objective was to understand the NEOD experience in the context of crisis innovation, decision-making, and motivation. Within this context, the following process articulated by Moustakas (1994) and Creswell (2013) are modestly followed:

- A phenomenon to be explored

- A group of individuals that have experienced the phenomenon

- A group of individuals that have experienced this phenomenon

- Bracketing of researcher experiences

- Data collection including interviews and observation

- Data Analysis seeking clusters of meaning

- Descriptive passage discussing the experiential essence focused on the "what" and the "how." (Creswell, 2013, pp. 78-81)

Moustakas (1994) recommended using two open ended questions to explore a phenomenon, but this study deviates from this generalized approach based upon the need to understand specific elements of the NEOD mindset phenomenon. Delving into focused areas of interest (innovation, decision making, motivation) may support the urgent global need to identify, recruit, build and retain NEOD personnel.

Bracketing of personal experience as an NEOD technician will be critical to "focus on the personal experiences of the participants" (Creswell, 2013, p. 78). Achieving researcher distance from ground operations, combined with an understanding of the bracketing challenge, may provide enough time, distance, and shielding to prevent data interference. The goal for this study is to capture the essence of the NEOD mindset experience without allowing experiential baggage to interfere (Giorgi, 1992, 1997).

Participants

Forward deployed (outside the Continental United States) NEOD personnel are selected for this research, because they are closest to the IED fight. The Pacific theater of operations based on geographic magnitude via the Department of Defense Pacific Commander (PACOM) supports approximately 50% of the global surface area and 5 of 7 U.S. treaty allies (http://www.pacom.mil, 2016). During the May 12-14, 2015 EOD conference Kuala Lumpur, Malaysia, a significant IED problem was noted across South Asia and Southeast Asia, in particular Bangladesh, India, Indonesia, Philippines, and Thailand (Frank, 2015). Furthermore, Asia is a significant global generator of emerging technologies, especially electronics, the driving mechanism of many IEDs. In simple terms, the Pacific theater is a huge area with a challenging IED problem and evolving technologies (Conflict Armament Research, 2016; https://www.usarpac.army.mil/apcied, n.d.).

Based upon security considerations, NEOD is difficult to access. Protecting the identity of personnel, operational activities of the past, present, and future are critical facets of dealing with this highly specialized segment of special operations (Banks, 2013). Fortunately, access and permissions to interview personnel were approved for this study provided transcripts strictly adhered to security classification procedures ensuring no operationally sensitive material would be included, nor would there be any recording of personal statements be produced. Senior leadership and security personnel had the option to read all materials prior to submission to ensure no operation would be put at risk or operators identified. The NEOD community was supportive, because the intended goal was to make things better for the NEOD technician, which could ultimately save more lives.

Creswell (2013) noted that phenomenological qualitative studies varied in sampling size from "1 to 325 participants, with most studies falling in between 10 and 30 participants" (p. 157). The sample size needs to be large enough to gain the appropriate data, but small enough not to become unwieldy (Moustakas, 1994). Morse (2000, 2015) provided extensive guidance on sample size selection with the primary objective being to gain enough data that identifies salient clusters to achieve saturation. Consequently, a total of 22 participants were selected to bisect skill levels in single iteration interviews. NEOD consists of three qualification standards: basic, senior, and master technician. Two intact teams (a team of 4, a team of 5) were also interviewed to understand innovation and decision making group processes. In this manner, the goal is to understand the phenomenon in question across skill levels, as well as from the individual and group perspective to gain saturation.

All participants were male, because there were currently no female NEOD operators forward deployed on the interview location. Participants ranged in age from ages 19-45 with an experiential range from 2 years to 28 years in the NEOD community. Educational backgrounds ranged from high school graduate to Master degree holders. The 22 participants were multi-culturally diverse. All participants were NEOD school graduates, forward deployed, and actively employed as bomb disposal technicians. At no time did the study interfere with active operations or preparations for active operations. All participants were volunteers and research was conducted in off duty hours. Far more than 22 subjects volunteered to participate. The 22 selected provided the best available blend available of skill level, experiential level in NEOD, age, and racial / ethnic identification to achieve Creswell's (2013) maximum available depth and diversity.

Data Collection

Security classification adherence and participant welfare will be carefully observed during all stages of this study. On August 1, 2016, all NEOD members on location received a 30-minute briefing describing this study and providing the approved pamphlet. Subsequent volunteers received a detailed informed consent form acknowledged by a signature. The researcher read the instructions from a script to both individuals and the teams. The pamphlet and informed consent form provided specific avenues available to participants if they felt harmed in any way by the study.

Both documents noted that a participant may discontinue participation at any point in the process. All data garnered will be maintained with the utmost confidentiality in a secure space under lock and key. Based upon the extremely sensitive role NEOD operators perform, no recordings or identifying information was included in the data set. All materials were reviewed by the to ensure no classified data is included. The researcher acted as the primary filter to screen out specific classified data regarding named operations, locations, and or other identifying information that could pose a future risk. Beneficence and ethical principles were used throughout the study to promote trustworthiness and harness the researcher's subjective self.

Individual subjects were asked 14 open ended questions over the course of 2 hours (see Appendix A). Team interviews took place over the course of 3 hours and included 7 questions (see Appendix B). Participants remained anonymous and were assigned a random alpha numeric designator, or self selected designator. No recordings took place to guard against a security breech (i.e. a participant inadvertently mentions a classified activity). The researcher instead took careful notes sans sensitive operational information.

Data Analysis

After reviewing the multiple phenomenology research processes outlined in Creswell (2013), as well as phenomenological research of Applebaum (2012), Colaizzi (1978), Englander (2012), and Polkinghorne (2012), the following process is a comprehensive phenomenological research method to develop the data collection plan (Creswell, 2013, p. 82):

1. Carefully review all transcripts multiple times to resonate with the participant experience.

2. Identify and isolate significant statements that apply directly to the areas of interest.

    Specifically, what statements pertain to innovation, decision making and motivation particularly through the use of heuristics. The researcher will remain open to possible identification of new areas of interest that may be subsets of larger themes. For example, there may be a variety of motivational mechanisms in place among NEOD technicians.

3. Determine the clusters of meaning, seek validation, locate discrepancies.

    By grouping significant statements, particularly *"rules of thumb"* concerning motivation, innovation, decision making, and possible opportunities to capture a sense of how subjects experience or perceive the aforementioned categories. Finding discrepancies and similarities amongst subjects may offer a better understanding of how self-identified cognitive characteristics can be grouped. When specific clusters are unclear, it will be necessary to re-engage subjects to expand upon what they experience.

4. Integrate the clusters of meaning into textural and

    structural description.

    Connecting and contextualizing the aggregated subject areas of NEOD innovation, decision making and motivation into comprehensive descriptions will provide insight into the NEOD experience. For example, describing all inputs concerning motivation and connecting them structurally into cohesive text will facilitate the identification of NEOD essence.

5. Isolate the invariant structure or essence.

    From the structural and textual review, a consistent framework and belief structure will be identifiable. Determining the essence of NEOD will be distilled through consolidation of interviews, isolation of meanings, and identification of invariable patterns.

Data was developed beginning with the tactical operator, the closest person to the point at which decision-making and crisis innovation take place. This is also the level in which first-hand knowledge of motivation can be gained as self-reported by the operator. Figure 2 provides a representation of the process scaffolding. These steps are repeatable across the global Explosive Ordnance Disposal enterprise because qualitative phenomenology is

77

proven to be credible and reliable (Creswell, 2013; Smith et al.,

2009).

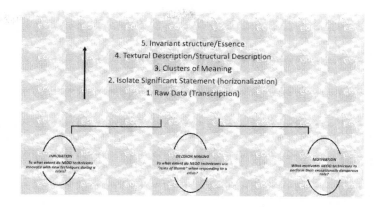

Figure 2: Illustration of phenomenological data analysis steps

To obtain the essence of the NEOD mindset phenomenon, it

was necessary to become completely immersed in the data recovered

(Smith, 2011A). Data collection was carefully transcribed, coded,

and sorted to identify patterns. Cognitive mapping technique

common to Integrative Phenomenological Analysis (IPA) was used

to provide descriptions (Smith, 2011B; Smith et al., 2009).

Garnering data verbally, reviewing transcripts and graphically

displaying information helped grasp the lived experience of NEOD

and provide a depiction of the NEOD experience.

Summary

Chapter Three included a description of the phenomenological qualitative research design that justified the need for this study based upon a constructivist perspective. Meaning is a product of worldview and social relationships. The phenomenological method provided data on the lived experience of the participants. The research design is an academically validated process that is reliable, credible, and suited to the goals of the research. Purposeful decisions regarding the number of participants, their skill levels, location of interviews, and locations of participants are complete. The research design was an efficient method to understand the NEOD mindset through the lens of crisis innovation, decision making, and motivation. Chapter Four includes a description of study participants, outlines qualitative interview results, and identifies emerging themes as they pertain to the research questions.

CHAPTER FOUR: RESULTS

This study explored how NEOD technician's experience their role in bomb disposal through a mindset focused on motivation, decision-making, and crisis innovation. A research gap exists in the field of bomb disposal and need for further research was identified (Bundy & Sims, 2007; Cooper, 1982; Hogan & Hogan, 1989). "IED's have emerged as the paradigmatic weapons of asymmetrical conflicts" (Revill, 2016, p. 60) and the primary counter to IEDs are bomb disposal technicians (Laska, 2015). Studying the scaffolding of how NEOD experiences and understands their activities revealed the significance NEOD places on mindset. This study used a phenomenological qualitative research design and culminated in an authentic perspective of NEOD lived experiences based on motivation, decision-making, and crisis innovation. To learn how NEOD technicians understand and experience bomb disposal, research focused on three fundamental questions:

1. To what extent do NEOD technicians innovate with new techniques during an EOD crisis response?

2. To what extent do NEOD technicians use *rules of thumb* when responding to a crisis?

3. What motivates NEOD technicians to perform their exceptionally dangerous role?

Chapter Four presents findings resulting from 13 individual interviews and 2 team interviews (*Team Tantalus*: 4 members; *Team Prometheus*: 5 members). All participants were fully qualified NEOD technicians and actively deployed performing bomb disposal activities. Using Integrative Phenomenological Analysis (IPA), word and thought patterns from participant transcripts were extensively reviewed to achieve immersion, identify themes, and isolate units of meaning (Smith, Flowers, & Larkin, 2009). Units of meaning were parsed into 28 clustered meaning subsets, eventually leading to identification of 13 themes.

Summary of Participants

Data was collected for this phenomenological study through face-to-face interviews of 13 individuals and 2 teams (n = 5, n = 4). Criterion sampling of fully operational and qualified NEOD technicians increased the probability of reaching motivated participants actively engaged in decision-making and crisis innovation under field conditions. All participants included had: (a) graduated from Naval Explosive Ordnance Disposal School (b) qualified as Naval Parachutists (c) qualified as Naval Divers (d) completed tactical training in weapons and hand-to-hand combat (e) successfully completed a 6-9 month pre-deployment team training and validation process; and (f) were presently, or previously engaged in responding to bomb disposal calls. Non-operational personnel were excluded.

The sample included all males because there were no female NEOD technicians available on location during the course of the study. Ages ranged from 23 to 41 years old and provided a range of NEOD qualification levels with: (a) 6 Officers, (b) 5 Master technicians (c) 7 Senior Technicians and (4) Basic technicians. One technician identified as being Hispanic and one technician identified with being multi-ethnic, while the remaining 20 identified as Caucasian. Military rank was spread across operational ranks with 6 Junior Officers (pay grade 03), 5 Non-commissioned Officers (pay grades E7-E9) and 11 Petty Officers (pay grades E6 and below).

Based upon security requirements of this study, participant names could not be used. Participants were offered the option of choosing their own informal naming convention or having a randomly assigned alpha numeric code. Dialog of participants below are identified in italics using either a randomly assigned code or self-selected identifier. Locations of events and specific operational data have also been removed to protect personnel. Transcript notes have been sanitized of all personal identifiers, operational details, and locations. Every effort has been made to capture the lived experience of the NEOD technician at the operational level.

Results Research Question One

IEDs, by definition, are improvised and rely upon malevolent creativity (Cropley, 2015) to develop unique design characteristics, deployment methods and actuation (Laska, 2015, Revill, 2016). NEOD responses to crisis are also frustratingly varied, ranging from: an explosive event, chemical, biological, or nuclear incident; diving, parachuting, rappelling; combat with enemy forces, multiple IEDs and hoaxes (U.S. Navy, 2016). Defeating a creatively built and deployed IED may require the NEOD technician to innovate in order to defeat the device. Consequently, Research Question One asked: To what extent do NEOD technicians innovate with new techniques during an EOD crisis response?

Theme One

Every EOD response is unique. 21 of 22 participants cited the unscripted nature of the NEOD response based on an entirely new problem set every time they respond. *Odin* noted that "there is no perfect set of procedures because every problem is unique." *Clam* said, "I have been doing this for more than 15 years and have not seen the same problem twice, that is why the EOD mindset is important, because (expletive) changes every time." *Juggernaut* advised, "Even the bad guys get a vote" on how they are going to "change the game right in the middle of the response" because "I have begun calls with one IED, find more, then civilians show up, and then some enemy snipers, and yeah, then Murphy gets involved (slang: inferring an unfortunate turn of events), and comms go down (slang: loss of communication capability)." *P4Product* noted, "so yeah, the hundred pound heads try to make a tool for every kooky problem, after the fact of course, but they don't get it, every problem is new and the response is how we think, not some widget." *X11* added, "Every problem is unique. From big picture to details."

Theme Two

Unique EOD responses require time critical innovation that includes networking, questioning, observing, experimenting, and connectional intelligence. 13 individual participants and both NEOD teams identified innovative responses in time limited problem sets. *Honeybear* was physically exhausted after numerous response calls in a high temperature environment and not eager to put on the cumbersome bomb suit. His team was responding to an training IED caught in the top of a fence because someone had attempted to throw it over the fence. This was a time critical problem, and *Honeybear*:

> took a long painters pole and connected a J-Knife and series of hooks on the end of the pole with zip ties and duct tape. Then I put the painter pole into the robot gripper, drove the robot down to the device, cut it from the fence with the J-knife, pulled it (the IED) off the fence with the hooks, and we took care of it.

In a similar crisis innovation, *X20* noted:

> I was under enemy sniper fire and trying to pull an IED away from an escape route, but after 6 IED responses in extreme heat, I was smoked (exhausted) and out of pull line (rope to

pull a device/person/thing away), so I grabbed a wad of spent non-el (non-electric firing tube, similar to aquarium tubing) and used that, it worked awesome. It probably wasn't the perfect answer, but it supported rule number one, beat the device and win.

X10 and his team responded to recover a corpse of drowned partner nation EOD technician. Traditional recovery attempts using divers had been unsuccessful because of extreme tides and currents, so the team opted to experiment with their underwater robot. *X10* was the Subject Matter Expert (SME) driving the robot and said:

The friggin current was ripping and we had been looking for this guy for a week. *P4Product* had ball parked (slang: estimated) where he thought the body might be from maps and currents, and through some unbelievable weirdness, we got a blip on the sonar, but the tide was shifting. I had about ten seconds to figure out what I was going to do and take action or that body would have been gone. I figured if I got ahold of the dive regulator hose that I could make the angle of the lift, in that current, moving a pretty good clip, it would work…and it did. Nobody could believe it. I am sure I broke a butt ton of rules from the tool manual specifications, but it got the job done.

X14 brought up the importance networking with people to innovate and respond to EOD problems. As an Officer of a specialized team, *X14* acts as the liaison between his team, partner countries, government agencies, civilians, and medical personnel. He noted:

> most of my innovations involve connecting with people to gain information or leverage actions, often rapidly. I have developed Humanitarian Mine Action programs in 7 countries, and observing people, assessing their motivations, and pushing their buttons to get urgent results is an art.

X11 also identified "networking with people is a key part of our innovation secret sauce." *X13* commented from a similar perspective:

> As the OIC (Officer In Charge), my job is to staff creatively as well as help work problems, most of the challenges we meet are because our solutions are so off the wall, getting an institutionalized leader to let my team run with an insanely unique solution is a staff problem. Innovating by gaining

permissions from traditionalists, or perhaps in some cases, dodging administrative land mines (slang: pitfalls) is a lot of fun. It is a game of wits.

Questioning the status quo and striving to "make it better" was cited by 12 of the 13 individual respondents and both teams. Questioning is often followed by unusual, and likely irregular experimentation in order to "get results" with all participants citing "product over process" and "saving lives" or "beating the device" as a primary goal. *Clam* and his previous team noted:

We responded to some Army guys that had the tire on their JERRV (Joint EOD Ready Response Vehicle) catch fire after being hit with an RPG (Rocket Propelled Grenade) and decided we did not need that big (expletive) tire on the back of the JERRV. It would be too heavy to change under attack and did not meet our needs, so we took it off. After we looked at the tire well, we thought man, it would be good to have some more armor plating back there, so we hooked up (slang: networked with) some dudes in the metal shop and figured out how to cut a half inch plate of steel and mount it where the spare tire had been. We knew we were safer and all the guys too scared to make their own adjustments were

envious of our modified JERRV. My whole team made it

back home alive, because we tried new stuff and made every

piece of kit, and every process better, at every opportunity.

P4Product described another JERRV experiment in a different area

of operations:

Yeah so the JERRV was sucking (functioning inadequately)

in the place we were working. Every time we got out some

rat bag was trying to kill us, so we became experts at

modifying the JERRV so that we could deploy equipment

without getting out of the vehicle unless absolutely necessary.

We made a bridle to reel our our firing wire and non-el, then

we built a rigging system that let us launch the robot from the

vehicle without opening the door, but as we kept improving,

we figured we would need to cut some openings into the

vehicle hull. So I went over to the vehicle shop and they told

me hell no, so I just took the plasma cutting torch, went back

to the shop and cut some holes and welded on a few mounts.

Our JERRV pretty much became the prototype and every

team that saw it made similar adjustments because it worked

and was a metric butt ton safer. The terrorists didn't care for it much 'cause it jammed up their bad boy game against us.

Juggernaut was often requested because of basic Arabic capability and ability to network with partner forces. *Juggernaut* noted:

> So being the only guy on my team with some Arabic, I was getting called out a lot, and it was hotter than 7 hells, so I was smoked (slang: exhausted). One of my jobs was to interview witnesses, ask questions, and keep my beady eyes open to what was going on. These local civilians kept wanting to walk me around through crazy areas to see an IED. I could see this was going to end up with me being pink mist (slang: body exploded by an IED), so I was like, hey man, I will use this laser sight on my gun and walk the laser down to the place you saw it, you tell me when I am on the spot where you saw the IED. As soon as the local bubba gave me a location with my laser mark, we just drove the robot to the spot and my survival stats jumped through the roof. You know, you have to think fast and think smart in this game or you won't make it.

Team Prometheus responded to a training Maritime IED (MIED) and wanted to stop it from floating into a populated area:

We had been out searching for hours when we finally got to this thing, and it was spooky but not sure how many we had. Rather than get jammed on a single item, we wanted to complete the search, keep these things away from people, and then beat all the devices. So we needed a way to harness them, in order to move them, and then we could beat them (defeat the device). So we had been fooling around with these pool noodles earlier in the day and thought wow, if we make a quick hula hoop with pool noodles and bungee cord, we can make a bra to put over the MIED and hold them in one spot, or tow them anywhere. Only took a few minutes and worked like a charm.

Team Tantalus was called to a high pressure EOD response requiring an X-Ray to determine if there was a dangerous liquid substance inside a container that had never been seen before. The container was of an odd shape and difficult to X-Ray, and had only 30 minutes available to access the location, take the X-Ray, and determine if there was liquid inside the container. *Team Tantalus* decided to:

> make a wrap around Velcro frame to mount the X-Ray, build
> a dummy device both with and without liquid to have a
> baseline to work from, and then go shoot (slang: take an X-
> Ray) the real device. That X-ray conclusively showed the
> problem was bullshit because the real device was empty.
> Nobody could figure out how the hell we made the shot, but
> they don't know we are bloody Velcro artists.

Another repeated theme regarding innovation was participant's universal belief that all tools have more than one job. *Clam* said, "a wrench isn't just a wrench, there are 10,000 uses for that thing, you just have to think outside the box, connect some dots and make it work." *X9* was trying to move a civilian casualty in the middle of a fire, "I looked at my buddy with a piece of webbing, realized I had webbing and made an improvised sling in about 30 seconds to make a sling and tote that guy right out of the game show (crisis event)." *Team Tantalus*:

> never wants to have a single use tool, we need multi-use
> items, because we can't anticipate what problem we will get,

only that it will be something we haven't seen before. You can't carry everything. Best tool to beat a bomb is our mindset.

Juggernaut recalled his team requiring a procedure to fire an explosive projectile through an IED, but not being able to obtain the desired angle for the tool:

We used frying pans with holes drilled through them at the desired angle to make a wall mounted tool stand and shoot the IED at the correct angle. Now they have a tool for it, but for us, we just figured we could build it and it would work, and it did. There just happened to be frying pans at the site and it was an easy fix, took about three minutes from concept to execution. You know, that's why you have to pay attention to everything, because all this stuff just laying around is another tool box.

Training for responses to EOD problems can be just as challenging as the response itself. *X14* had a potentially devastating parachuting mishap:

I had a parachute cutaway (slang: main parachute failed to function) at 2500 hundred feet, and was good to go by 2000 feet, but I was way the hell off target (when landing). Problem was, I was too calm on the radio and the guys listening thought I was joking, so took forever to get picked up. The pick up crew figured that I would be freaked out after the cutaway, but man, we train to connect the dots (slang: trouble shoot problems), and death can be an outcome, no need to get all giddy about it.

Honeybear experienced a diving rig malfunction 120 feet under the sea that required crisis innovation:

I was having trouble breathing and went through the emergency procedures but the textbook fix (slang: official procedure) only lasted a few minutes before I would have difficulty breathing again, and I was in the process of aborting the dive (returning to surface) but needed some decompression time (divers require time to off gas to ascend safely). So I am connecting the dots on all this stuff going wrong, and moving towards the Emergency Breathing System (EBS) when Murphy strikes 'cause the EBS is down (not functioning) and its starting to get fun with my tunnel vision from lack of 02 (Oxygen), so I thought hey its either

I'm toast or time to connect some dots and take action, so I did this funky move to flip on my back, hit the surface and rip off my mask as I passed out. Guys pulled me in the boat and I puked a while but in the end, good to go, that's why they call me the *cockroach of the sea*. You have to know the rules to break them, and they found out later there was a one-way valve equipment failure, so if I hadn't made a plan in jacked up conditions, I'd be fish bait (slang: dead in the ocean). I was out of Schlitz (slang: lacking capacity).

Innovate or die, baby.

Theme Three

Crisis innovation is a component of NEOD mindset and taught in the NEOD community. *X20* detailed a reflective analysis of the NEOD training and innovation experience:

The foundation for innovation is established at the EOD school where a level of mastery is gained through progressive learning because the intense speed you are taught forces you to compound knowledge. You can call it a lot of different things, but the main thing is to make safe decisions quickly. We formulate a foundation in school and innovation improves with experience and coaching, especially if you have the right kind of team make up.

X11 further explained the NEOD innovation experience:

If you are not always innovative you will get weeded out. The innovations have to be practical and work, this is not some creative baloney, this is pink mist (slang: death by detonation), so you observe everything around you and choose fast, then you put your (expletive) on the line. We are taught innovation through trial and error until it becomes second nature.

Clam similarly noted:

We start by learning all the rules and then figuring out which ones we can break and when, we seek results, so doesn't much matter how you beat a problem as long as you were safe. The right answer in bomb disposal is the one that works. We also learn to try new stuff and ask a lot of questions. It's a thinking man's game.

P4Product's perspective was similar:

EOD school provides entry to market tools, but then you need experience. The best we can do is get the guys an insanely diverse set of skills, then expose them to all kinds of challenges, and get them to the game show (slang: actual EOD responses). Over time, they learn the right answer is the one that works. It doesn't need to look pretty or impress anyone.

Odin noted the importance of problems being time limited:

Time constraints force innovation, so timed problems build the skills, we also train in school to think critically with small teams working together while ignoring formal rank structure. This fuels innovation. Failure with a possibility of death is pretty motivating. It doesn't matter how you beat a problem....you just have to beat it...and if you don't, it bites back (slang: the IED hurts you). We have *skin in the game* (slang: at personal risk), so there is a fair amount of interest in *getting at it* (slang: impetus to achieve results).

Innovation was identified as a culturally shared process in the NEOD mindset. *Juggernaut* said:

We teach innovation because we are always open to working in mixed skill teams and using new ideas. We also spend a lot of time telling sea stories about calls (slang: EOD responses) and how we played it. We trade, network and broker every kind of knowledge. We share knowledge of how we innovated on problems to win, in fact we (expletive indicating emphasis) glorify it. New solutions are always sought because every problem is unique. This is a game free of rules, you just have to be safe. It's as hardcore as it gets and we reach across a (expletive) ton (slang: extensive) of technology, knowledge, skills, and abilities.

Honeybear expanded on the experience of innovation within NEOD:

We breed innovation, but most guys attracted to this are innovative to begin with, guys learn a lot from sharing experiences. I learn something every time I watch a drill in RNT (slang: Readiness and Training department), and see how innovative it is because every team may solve the problem successfully, but use a completely different process. Being on a team with other innovators is fuel to the fire, we are like *the Google of the Navy.*

Interestingly, *X9* noted the ability to innovate in crisis did not extrapolate to administrative duties:

I am innovative, and I know my strengths and weaknesses, but I work better under stress. In extreme circumstances I am really innovative, but behind a desk, I am not innovative. NEOD teaches innovation. We have x tools, y problem and need z results. We are trained to solve dangerous problems, highly complex and challenging problems. The best innovation comes when you have general parameters like beat the device, and not enough time to get the job done. If you want a written report, talk to somebody else.

The closing statement on NEOD confidence was delivered best by *X11*, "We never believe we will be beat, even when the cards are down."

Theme Four

NEOD technicians reported egalitarian teams with broad diversity in rank, experience and interests help them succeed. The diversity in personal and professional skill sets among the 22 participants was unusual. 8 of the 22 participants identified NEOD as the *Google of the Navy*, with X14 providing an innovative

description of the NEOD technician's as "bohemian athletic nerds,

prone to tenacity and aggressive altruism." 21 of 22 participants

interviewed were on a team constructed of (a) an NEOD Officer

(Lieutenant; Officer in Charge, OIC) between 25-30 years old,

holding at least a Bachelors degree, (b) a seasoned Non-

Commissioned Officer (Chief-Senior Chief-Master Chief) Master

EOD Technician (*Master Blaster*), (c) 1-3 Senior EOD technicians

(Petty Officers), and (d) 1-2 Basic EOD technicians (Petty Officers).

When an EOD task is delegated to the team via the Officer, *Team

Prometheus* said:

> The OIC takes all the info, shares useful data with the team
>
> *collars in* (slang: no rank or titles used), give them all a look
>
> at any pictures and team ensures all tools are up (slang:
>
> operational) by known specialty area. Once all tool checks
>
> are good, the team throws out a bunch of ideas. The Master
>
> Blaster is like a quality control guy, *he doesn't have to have
>
> the right answer, he just has to know what right looks like.*
>
> We have open dialog all the way to the scene, where we re-
>
> assess, determine a course of action as a team and *get at it.*

Team Tantalus identified their egalitarian process upon receiving a tasking as:

> The OIC gives a quick hash (slang: review key points) on the gig, everyone knows their role and probably looks like nothing from the outside other than a functioning machine. We are naturally on the same page as we have spent 6-12 months working up for deployment together. We pretty much ignore Navy protocol on the team when working internally because it adds artificial barriers. Its really critical to identify key features of the problem and exchange information quickly, without bullshit. The *Master Blaster* makes the final safety calls, but otherwise does not say much as he watches the team develop on a problem set, and the Officer deals with staff weenies. Anyone can interject new information or an idea at any time. Anyone on the team can stop what's happening for a safety issue as well. We operate as a flat organization.

The skill sets outside of work in the NEOD community are diverse. *Team Tantalus* said:

Our team is extremely diverse. Everyone has a job, a life and a something on the outside that is completely disparate from the others. From computer languages to radiation physics or physiology, we all have a different skill and focus, so when we come together, it's a rodeo to win.

The sheer diversity of team skills was rather surprising during the interview process. There were (a) two classical Cello musicians (one wait listed to Julliard), (b) a competitive slack liner (tight rope walking between buildings or cliffs), (c) four competitive sport parachutists, (d) 21 out of 22 participants practiced competitive physical activity (Body Building, Ultra-Marathon, Cross Fit, Extreme Swimming, Judo, Karate, Jujitsu, Mixed Martial Arts), (e) 6 robotics and space engineering specialists, (f) 4 computer programmers, (g) 14 yoga practitioners, (h) 11 dirt bike racers, (j) a former inner city paramedic, (k) 16 foreign language students, (l) 1 coloring book aficionado, (m) 4 world events and strategic foreign policy students, (n) one military history buff, (7) trained chefs, and (p) 3 beer brewers. This is certainly a partial listing because as two of the Officers noted:

We get a call, and I shout into the work space, hey who can do XYZ? And some guy always yells back they know how to do XYZ. Just when I think I have seen it all the team has, I learn something new. Last year, I was in a remote foreign location, at the local tavern, with two teams letting off some steam. There was a dance band from a large metropolitan city and they announced a dance contest. Turns out, one of my peers was literally a ranked competitive ballroom dancer. We kicked their ass. You can't make this stuff up. These guys get interested in something, spend two years learning all about it, and then move on, so you never know what's next.

Individually, participant *X11* captured the *athletic bohemian nerd* essence when he described his personal interests, "I play the saxophone and piano. Enjoy painting, drawing, hunting and fishing. I will do everything possible with a professional coach and deliberate practice to become good, but once I am competitive, I move to a new skill."

Competition was a common theme throughout 19 interviews. During individual interviews, participants regularly captured their desire to *win* or *beat the device. X20's* commentary was representative of competitive advantage through diversity:

> Its kind of weird, so there may be 5 or 8 guys on your team, but these guys are a long way from average. Each guy has all these tech abilities, different educational background and some kind of bat shit crazy skills. When we have time, we all pursue our off the wall interests, *sort of like Google guys*, but then when we get to a problem set (slang: EOD response), and we come together as a team, the strength of our collective knowledge is unreal. We question everything, try new stuff out, and focus on winning, or even talk to anyone, in any industry. Big Daddy Navy gives us, like a hippie mom and dad, (slang: inference Officer and Chief oversight), but otherwise, they let us run wild. We just have to produce results when the time comes. If winning isn't part of your vocab, NEOD probably isn't for you.

Theme Five

NEOD technicians reported exceptional levels of confidence individually and in teams. During the interview process, teams expressed an unexpected level of emotion regarding their confidence to succeed in EOD response. *Team Prometheus* said, "we are 150% confident we can crush anything you send our way because we have done it. With think faster and better." *Team Tantalus*, in a separate interview noted, "we are 100% confident, we can handle anything and take on any terrorist out there. We have beaten every (expletive) device sent our way." Confidence was also a theme in 13 out of 13 individual interviews. *Honeybear* said, "no doubt, we can beat any device you send our way," while *X13* noted, "I am extremely confident if I am with my team, we train to together live together and count on each other to stay alive. It is a crazy bond. We can beat anything together." *Clam*, a vastly experienced Master EOD technician with deployments across the globe was a bit more reflective, but still exuded a quiet confidence:

> Very confident because the experience and deliberate training. I will protect personnel and property, and after that, hopefully my team and then myself. I don't have all the answers, but my team can come up with a lot of ideas, and more importantly, turn ideas into action on a dime. The most important tool we have is the EOD mindset, how you apply the thousands of technological tools we have is entirely

adaptable. I love a timed challenge, give me a problem and my team will figure it out.

When *X20*, an experienced Master EOD technician was queried on his confidence level, he noted:

> I am 150% confident we can win in any EOD response by beating the device. We train so far beyond the current problem set and so utterly outside the box that real world problems can get boring. We innovate to win and can manage as many variables as the bad guys throw at us.

Interestingly, NEOD confidence was reported in 10 out of 13 individual cases to be a product of teamwork, with the term *we* used rather than *I*. *Juggernaut* said:

> Not gonna let my alligator mouth speak for my rabbit arse (slang: infers humbleness), and understand our caps and lims (slang: capabilities and limitations), but I am very (expletive) confident my team can defeat whatever you send our way, or at least stop the civilian casualties. But its tricky, the day you think you know everything, its time to get out. Not saying we know all the answers, but we know all the rules and can figure stuff out in real time, because we are a badass team.

Overconfidence kills so we rely on each other, but under-

confidence never gets to the fight.

X15 discussed the importance of collaborative thinking and

the impact of working in

team before providing a unique response: "yeah, well,

hmmm…confident, yeah, *confident enough to bet your life and mine*

that I can beat the device." *P4Product* said, "I am extremely

confident that my team can beat anything with everyone's inputs…

very confident. Worst case, we will save a lot of lives before a few

of us pink mist." X14 said, "My team is the best, if its my team and

we can run the job, we can beat the device. Biggest threat is

management over-riding a field decision." *X9* expressed, "Absolute

confidence in my team to pull off a job (slang: EOD response), we

are all innovative thinkers. Highly confident in my mind. My team

is totally good to go (slang: competent)."

Research Question One Summary

NEOD technicians in this study (n = 22) report extensive use

of technology when innovating, much of it not used as originally

designed. From underwater robot adaptions for corpse recovery to

frying pans as a mounting system for precision explosive charges,

NEOD innovates. NEOD reports that the EOD responses they are called to are always unique, and as such, requires an innovative response. Participants reported crisis innovation as a component of an identifiable NEOD mindset. Innovation as a component of the EOD mindset is taught at the entry level in NEOD school, within the community after graduation, and through sharing of data. NEOD participants reported egalitarian team interaction with broad diversity in rank, experience and interests. NEOD participants preferred to win by defeating explosive threats and believe exceptionally diverse teams provided a competitive advantage help them succeed. NEOD participants reported exceptional levels of confidence, particularly when working in a team.

Results Research Question Two

To what extent do NEOD technicians use *rules of thumb* when responding to a crisis?

EOD responses are exceptionally diverse and the rigorous training process from new entrant to master EOD technician requires 5 to 10 years of focused practice, with some members never achieving the title of *Master Blaster* (Bundy & Sims, 2007; Cooper, 1982; Laska, 2015; Revill, 2016; U.S. Navy, 2016). Consolidating complex technologies and processes using heuristics has been studied within medicine and gambling (Gigenrenzer, 2007). Identifying what, if any, rules of thumb NEOD uses was the focus of research question number two.

Theme One

NEOD participants were extremely focused on defeating explosive devices and saving lives, but articulated heuristics that emphasized avoidance of rigid structural protocols and standardization of activities. 22 of 22 NEOD participants used the rule "you have to know the rules to break them" indicating mastery of the equipment as designed, or processes as delegated by higher authorities are guidelines, not rigid adherence to any structure. Another reported NEOD participant (22 of 22) rule of thumb was "do whatever it takes as long as it is safe, the right solution is the one that defeats the device." The final two rules of thumb universally supported by NEOD participants were "outcomes over process" and "product over process." Numerous other rules of thumb were reported by participants with less frequency.

Theme one was supported with several reported rules of thumb pertaining to innovative thinking. 19 participants reported they "need to think outside the box" with 16 noting they "live outside the box." 12 participants went reported they "don't even have a box" and they try to avoid anything that might interfere or cause them to "get tunnel vision." *X20* noted:

I hate it when we start getting all kinds of extraneous opinions from somebody that doesn't know what they are talking about because it distracts us from the cold hearted objective assessment necessary to be fast and furious. I trust hard data, the more the better, but when some bubba is trying to tell me useless background info, I shut him down. It really drives me nuts when they tell me I need some special tool to execute an obscure task when I know my team will figure it out with our multi-use tools and mad hatter team. Its like hey dude, don't put me in a box. We are free range chickens and we always deliver, juts get me to the problem.

Conversely, 14 participants noted how much they valued the opinion of qualified NEOD technicians unfamiliar with a new problem set, or opinions of recent entries into the NEOD field because they add a "fresh set of eyes." Master EOD Technician

P4Product noted:

> I dig having some young officer and white hats (slang: junior
>
> enlisted, E1-E6) on the team because they provide a *fresh set*
>
> *of eyes* on the problem. You know, after you have done a
>
> few 100 IEDs (training and real), you start to get stuck in a
>
> rut, and they start to look like a previous response you might
>
> have had. Tunnel vision kicks in because last time there was
>
> something your brain recorded. So I let the youngsters run
>
> wild and have them tell me what they see from their
>
> experience, and this helps us a get a better objective picture
>
> of what we are dealing with. My job is to build Master
>
> Blasters, and that comes from getting my bubbas time on
>
> target doing the deed. I don't have to have the answer as the
>
> Master Blaster, I just have to know what right looks like.
>
> When I say right, I mean its safe, and will probably work.

Theme Two

NEOD technician's relationship to their high value

equipment is intense. *X14* noted, "So I have something like $5 million of equipment in my shop, but the kit is useless if not

maintained, ready to go, and with an expert operator." 22

participants repeated the rule of thumb, "if you take care of your

gear, your gear will take care of you." 21 participants identified

their gear as "life support equipment" and "the difference between

dead or alive" inferring that if the gear does not function, the risk of

death increases. *Honeybear*, an experienced senior EOD technician

said:

> That's the deal on being a senior tech, you need to know
>
> every single piece of gear inside and out, from explosive
>
> tools to diving and parachuting gear. There are 10s of
>
> thousands of data points. As the senior tech, I am the gear
>
> guy, and my gear needs to be always ready, always pampered,
>
> and I need to know everything about it. I'm not sure if
>
> civilians can understand this one, but if my gear is down, we
>
> might not be able to get to the sea mine or IED, and they (the
>
> explosive device) might kill a lot of people. My friends back
>
> home say yeah, we know about this or that motorcycle
>
> engine or something, but they don't get it, this gear is life or
>
> death. When you really know your gear, you also know how

to use it in unorthodox ways, so you gotta know *what rules you can break*, but you will never know if you don't understand the kit.

Another feature demonstrating 22 of 22 NEOD participant's attachment to their equipment were the rules of thumb that identify the attachment, "never break up your kit" or "never separate your equipment." *X11* captured the reasons clearly:

Guys that don't understand our role always have some good idea fairy landing about the gear. Sometimes the (other service) supply guys will decide they want to send stuff in a few shipments, or someone will decide there is not enough space and want to spread gear into multiple locations. But if we don't have the gear with us and ready to go, we have no capability. My new guys sometimes show up and are in a bit of shock, because I need guys to be ready at all times, with kit ready at all times. A crisis is not a pick up game. When the team needs you and the kit, you better be ready, your kit better be ready, or we will have problems. Somebody always stays with the gear, we don't just leave it hoping that it gets on a plane and shows up with a receipt. That would be bush league.

22 of 22 NEOD participants recited the important operational rule of thumb, "two is one, one is none" because (X9) "high tech gear is finicky and if the first piece of kit fails, we need another ready to go."

Theme Three

NEOD decision-making is linear in early portion of their career, but as they gain experience, it becomes more intuitive. *X13* noted:

At the beginning levels, checklists are necessary. We have to review rules with a list and apply the rules, but as time goes on and these rules are internalized, *we know what rules we need to break and why*. This is a team activity. The Master Blaster sharp shoots (slang: acts as safety advisor), but we all work as equals and then execute. We are driven by the situation through elevating levels of threat assessment. Anyway, as experience grows, we move through the decision process using quick rules of thumb and an internal checklist.

Honeybear experienced the check off list versus internalized rules of thumb in an underwater emergency:

Me and my dive buddy Ginger were diving super deep trying to attach a lift balloon (remotely initiated inflatable balloon that allows lifting of heavy objects from the bottom of the ocean), to an unexploded bomb on a reef. The current was pulling us all over and we were getting pretty beat up, and the visibility was about 6 inches, so I couldn't see anything. Ginger got to the bomb first, so he dragged me over to the bomb so we could attach the lift balloon, and snapped me into a lug so I could work on the dang thing, but I didn't know it at the time. But it did seem a lot easier to get to work, I just thought the current died down. Then Ginger's dive rig starts to act goofy, and he has to go, so I am there working on the bomb, and finish up the rigging the lift balloon. I try to ascend, but I didn't realize I was snapped into this thing, because I can't see anything by now and I have kicked up all the mud working. Hmmm, wonder what the deal is, and start walking through my check off list…got nothing. Then I remember, Ginger is a Master Blaster, he must have done something I didn't quite follow when he snapped me in, so I start to trace out my line, find where I am snapped in, and good to go. Back to the dive boat and happy. But it made me think, I am a senior tech, sort of a journeyman, but still really locked into checklists, but I could see that working with a more experienced guy, he was making common sense calls to get the job done. Digital and analog thinking brother.

The Master EOD technicians (4 of 4) reported the need to methodically move through problems with the first rule of thumb being "what can kill me now." *Clam* explained:

When I started out of school I needed to go slow and use a checklist. As I gained experience I developed or internalized a threat assessment matrix that helped me make good decisions quickly. I prioritize threats into *what can hurt me now* and continue to shoot those ducks (slang: resolve). A checklist gets you out the door, but attention to detail, the connecting of different variables into your threat assessment keep you alive. Our guys need to connect the dots and prioritize. Easiest priority is *what can kill me right*

(expletive) now?

X20, another Master EOD technician with extensive combat

experience explained his

view of threat assessment and rules of thumb:

> Coming out of EOD school, I was always going
>
> through check off sheets. Once a team leader, then
>
> you have to see the big picture. On my second pump
>
> (slang: deployment) in Iraq, we did a lot of OJT (On
>
> the Job training) to add skills to the box (slang:
>
> adding personal skills to a mental toolbox). The best
>
> piece of advice I give to the new guys as a rule of
>
> thumb is to *always think three steps ahead of where*
>
> *you are at.* As a new guy, you only understand what
>
> you see and the list. As you get your game together
>
> over time and become a team leader use your
>
> checklist in your brain to stay 3 steps ahead. Good
>
> Master Blasters are 4 steps ahead before a call even
>
> goes down. Gotta keep safety protocols, because
>
> something is surely trying to kill you now, an IED, a

sniper, or even a slip up from our end. The new EOD guy is thinking about what he is doing now, the Master Blaster is putting it all together and asking questions. Do I have air cover to stop bad guys shooting at me? Can I do a detonation in 15 minutes, who is nearby? Do I have enough demo (slang: explosive material) to respond to X number of calls after this? How much battery life on the robots left? Can I do a call on the way back to base, or will I be out of demo and out of battery juice?

Master EOD technician *P4Product* shared his decision making rules of thumb:

> As a beginner everything is scary, so much data, working of checklists, too hard to anticipate what is needed. As time goes on and multiple deployments pass, the ability to develop an internalized rule set follows. Builds the ability to internalize knowledge of threat assessment into a layered approach that is a progressive threat assessment process. It is both *fast and expedient*. The timed nature of the problem also

adjusts or scales to every situation, sometimes you have time, sometimes you don't, but I need to regulate myself and the response. The days of of a single IED response are rare, we may need to work 18 hours straight on through multiple events, its important to move at the right pace so we have enough juice. Don't want to run out of Schlitz (slang: capacity). Key rule of thumb is to *be agile, scalable, fast.*

Juggernaut, an experienced Senior EOD technician under preparation for his 30 day Master Blaster board exam, reiterates a similar theme on threat prioritization and rules of thumb:

Everything depends upon the category or urgency of the problem, *we never say never or always,* we adjust our process based on the problem set. If we have time, check off sheets are useful, but when its timed and urgent, we need to move out with some well known rules and *get er done.* The big question is *what can kill me now,* fix that and move on to the next thing that *can kill me now.* I dial in (slang: adjust based on situation) the process that I have time for….slow and deliberate if it allows, but screaming through the air at 140mph (parachuting) there isn't a lot of time to debate the steps. When a plan deviates, we fix the problem and then return to the plan. Prioritize and take action when getting shot at, and then return to the plan. Have to ask yourself, now what is the most important thing?

4 of the less experienced NEOD participants identified commonalities in the use of check list versus intuitive decision-making processes:

(X15) In the beginning, I used checklists and the rules taught at EOD school. Over time, I internalized the rules and identified some of my personal pitfalls: mainly to resist temptation to just solve a problem independently. I always remember, *fast is slow, and slow is fast.*

(X11) I used check off sheet of standard rules starting out, and they are still valuable when we have time. But now, in more urgent situations, I'm in a much stronger position to size up situation quickly and run

through all the basics, from general to specific. You really have to ask a lot of questions to get at the right data.

(*X10*) When you get to understand this business, it is really a series of simple steps buried in a highly charged and snotted up environment, reeling back to the ground truth is important. My Chief always tells me, *slow is smooth, smooth is fast.*

(*X14*) In the beginning it is linear and I needed to use a checklist. It is effective as parts of the whole become internalized. Team input of everyone regardless of rank is critical. This gives us a picture of from guys with fresh eyes, a very experienced NCO, and a young officer with a lot of technical background. We thrive on the team interaction and get flashes of input that are awesome. Once we concur on a plan, we use it until something better comes along, then regroup and re-attack. Situations are fluid, every problem is unique and evolves in unusual ways. As time goes on, we internalize an expedite rules, then adjust as needed quickly and efficiently.

(X9) I had a large amount of stressful decision-making processes in the past, rules are guidelines and you still have to move faster than you can read. You constantly have to size up a situation, constantly reassessing, *what's gonna kill me, what's gonna kill guys around me, what is going to kill innocents.* As time has gone on, I have less thinking consciously about decisions, just becomes internalized. Now, I no longer have to think about it, same deal in medicine, size it up…assess, act, re-assess…get to the angle that wins. *Get to the win, save lives.*

Theme Four

NEOD participants used heuristics to synthesize complex operational and technical concepts. All 22 participants identified "timed problems" as particularly challenging because there are extensive operational, technical, and administrative functions involved in every EOD response. Master EOD technician *Clam* noted:

As the team ancient Master Blaster, one of the things I need to help my new guys do is share tribal wisdom. When I was a new guy in combat, my Chief told me, *muddy boots are better than bloody boots* because he didn't have time for a long discussion to explain that bad guys were putting IEDs in well worn paths to kill us. He just gave us a simple phrase and we stayed the hell off the main path. There is a certain brilliance in those types of rules. Some of the others I like are *fresh eyes are good, just win,* and *tango's* (slang: terrorists) *don't take a day off* or *tango's don't waste time on BS.* The most important point is to *make it better* because we can improve every single thing we do to give us competitive advantage.

Master EOD technician *P4Product* shared rules of thumb that he shares with his teams:

My team can improve anything, and it needs to be constant. I am not too interested in hearing about challenges, so I use *don't give me problems, give me solutions,* and when they don't have a perfect solution, I share the NEOD mindset mantra of *make it better.* Sometimes we just get wrapped around the axel (slang: overly focused on unimportant details) and we all remind each other than *every problem is unique, every solution is unique.* Another thing that can easily get in the way is ego. Some communities are all jammed up over their legend, especially in SOF (Special Operations Forces), but that is definitely not us, because tooting your horn slows down decisions. If my team starts any social posturing, we call each other out with the rule of *don't be a hot dog.* We don't have a hot dog culture; we have an athletic nerd culture that *produces* in the shadows. Another unusual rule of thumb my Chief Master Blaster taught me 15 years ago (and his Master blaster taught him 40 years ago) was *Dead Man's Hand.* When the time comes to make the long walk downrange to an IED or something else that will kill you, we need to remember that even when everything seems perfect, you might pink mist out (slang: death by detonation). *Dead Man's Hand* was the final card game Wild Bill Hickok played when a coward came up behind his back and killed him. Wild Bill had a great hand of black Aces and Eights, things were going awesome for him

124

as one of the fastest gunfighters in the West, and then it was over. You will see a lot of our guys with *Dead Man's Hand* ink (slang: tattoo). Finally, my team mantra is *be a lion*, because we need to be bold, decisive, and fearless.

Basic and Senior EOD technicians shared their rules of thumb about NEOD gear, people, and operations:

(*Odin*) This probably sounds a little weird, but when I was at EOD school, there was this Swedish EOD guy in the international class with a lot of EOD experience and he had rules of thumb tattooed on his arms, so I started asking him about them, and the one that stuck with me was, *assumption is the mother of all* (expletive) *ups*. He talked to me about having *fresh eyes* on a problem and the issue in NEOD of assumptions being fatal. It has stuck with me, and we use it a lot, in closed groups of course. A few years later, I was working for a salty old Master Blaster, and he looked at my demo shot set up (slang: the explosive placement of demolition materials) and he let out an audible snort and said it "looks like crap." I said, yeah but it will work, and he intellectually punched my EOD pride, "yeah slick bomb (slang: term for an EOD beginner based on insignia), but this is not a timed problem, so you could *make it better* because *clean demo is good demo.* I changed my ways and use the same rules with my guys.

(*Juggernaut*) A lot of this gear is like you know, uber techie and then our tasks are completely varied and time dependent. Underwater work is time limited and you have to get to the surface, parachuting is really time constrained before you splat like a bug, and IED responses tend to be time limited. So I spend a lot of time telling my guys to *dial it in*, meaning they need to adjust the speed of whatever they are doing to match a problem.

In this business, we learn quick on high tech gear, like do I have 2 minutes to do a 30 minute set up for the kit, or four hours? More time can be better most of the time, but not always, because if you have too much time, the good idea fairy starts landing (slang: good ideas that are not practical). I tell my guys daily, *no good idea fairies*, I mean I dig new ideas, but the idea has to be actionable. Another thing I like to tell them about gear is after they tell me the gear is up (slang: prepared for use), I ask, *will you bet your life on it*, because that's the harsh reality.

(X11) As a newer guy, I can still remember most details from my EOD responses and sometimes talk about them with friends over drinks. Funny thing is, when you come into this EOD game, you hear a lot of rules of thumb, but they don't have much meaning, just seems like the dinosaurs rambling. But then when a crisis really happens, the rules make sense. My Chief had told me in the past, *low and slow for talking on the radio or briefing*, and *no drama queens on the X*, but it had no impact on me until I was in the fight. Then I watched as guys not used to this stuff (EOD response), and they were too scared to talk clearly on the radio and made it sound like they were not in control. Then we had a whole bunch of freaked out people near the incident site and in the CP (slang: Command Post) and I remembered the rules, got the drama queens out of the mix and the excited guy off the radio. Things worked a lot better after that because we need to think calmly and methodically.

Research Question Two Summary

NEOD participants were extremely focused on defeating explosive devices and saving lives, but articulated heuristics that emphasized avoidance of rigid structural protocols and standardization of activities. Participants universally reported use of heuristics to support results more than processes. The NEOD technician's relationship to their high value equipment is intense and participants identified use of heuristics about EOD tool use. NEOD participants articulated their decision-making process as linear in the early portion of their career, but as they gain experience, decisions become more intuitive. NEOD participants also used heuristics to synthesize complex operational and technical concepts. Use of heuristics by participants across the aforementioned broad range of NEOD activities, indicates probable utility for rules of thumb in the bomb disposal field.

Results Research Question Three

Gollwitzer (1999) noted motivation is a "primary cause of behavior" (cited in Smelser & Baltes, 2001, p.10109). Kotler (2014) identified avoiding death as the "most primary of primary drives" (p.

15). NEOD participants in this study chose to enter a high risk occupation where death is a common outcome of the activity. Hence, NEOD motivation, the primary cause of behavior may be a significant force in overcoming the most primary of primary drives, avoiding death. Motivation has been described as multidimensional (Petri & Govern, 2013), facilitated by purpose, autonomy, and mastery (Gillard, Gillard, & Pratt, 2015; Pink, 2009), or driven by the optimal feeling of *flow* (Csikszentmihalyi, 1990). From the perspective of positive psychology, understanding why NEOD operators opt to enter this dangerous all volunteer occupation, supports determining an answer to Research Question Three: What motivates NEOD technicians to perform their exceptionally dangerous role?

Theme One

NEOD participants were strongly motivated by a self-identified sense of purpose.

18 study participants noted their need for meaning and impact:

(X15) I was bored out of my mind in community college, it just seemed like an aimless and meaningless life. I wanted impact and meaning, you know to do something good in this world that was interesting. I was thinking about being a frogman (SEAL) and then my Uncle came home on leave and he was an EOD guy. Yeah, like what are the odds. He said I could do all the stuff SEALs do like shooting, diving and parachuting, but add something more technical like bomb disposal. He said it was a thinking man's game. He wasn't kidding, NEOD is all it's cracked up to be, we get to do everything cool and save lives. It really provides me with a purpose in life.

(*X14*) This is a volunteer force so guys volunteer for this because they they tend to be smarter than average, athletic, self motivated, altruistic. They have also see wealth and poverty but fall some place in between. Our reference point is to contribute to the greater good. We can work on problems we see as relevant and valued by society. We have the ability to make meaningful change with tremendous impact. Another key point is we are very small supporting component of SOF (Special Operations Forces) world in a weird way, so we always play second fiddle to the well known SEALs or Green Berets. NEOD tries harder, stays humble, and off the grid by design. We do all the things straight stick (slang: average) SOF guys do, plus our job of disarming bombs, when we get to the show (slang: incident site), but rarely take public credit. We are like some *Google element of the Navy* that trends toward bohemian athletic nerds.

(*X13*) Ok, so no giggling (slang: jokes about Naval Academy graduates are common), I hate talking about this stuff, but I went to the Naval Academy and we had to go on summer cruises to try and figure out what we wanted to do in the Navy. I was kind of a musical nerdy athlete, so lots of options were available. I visited all kinds of units and teams until we went to meet a SOF EOD team led by legendary and brilliant badass, Chris Mosko (Killed in Action, Afghanistan, 2012). Meeting Chris and that team was the most was the most unique, diverse, innovative and doctrinally independent unit I had ever seen. One taste of that nectar and I just had to be part of EOD because the purpose is altruistic and job has massive impact. Of course then once you get to the show, it's like catnip (slang: roughly equivalent to flow). In the last 6 months, I went jumping, diving, shooting and worked programming a new piece of underwater technology. What a rush, what an honor.

(*P4Product*) I watched the second Twin Tower fall while working as a journeyman electrician in NYC and it pissed me off on a lot of levels. I wondered what meaning my life had for the greater good, how I could have impact. I wanted to be a warrior, to do something impactful and altruistic, but what, medicine or EOD? EOD could save more lives, bigger impact and greater diversity in job, working out, parachuting diving, shooting, demolition. All the activity made this an easy choice and I wanted some skin in the game, 'cause what is a belief if you don't put skin in the game, I'll tell ya, its an opinion. I know EOD is the right thing for me to do.

(*X11*) I worked for a year making pretty good money but was bored to death. There was no impact or purpose to my life. I wanted something challenging, altruistic and meaningful. I wanted to have impact. I wanted to become a warrior, but the type of warrior with technical skills, and well rounded. NEOD is the thinking man's warrior, and I dig it.

(*X10*) I wasted a lot of time at college, because it was just weak sauce (slang: not useful). College seemed like a holding cell and was boring, like I was studying to gain a boring skill to go on to a boring life. So I tried to figure out what would give me meaning. I wanted to help people, be a warrior, do something athletic, and something technical. My first look at an Internet Video about EOD blew me away. It was love at first bite, EOD is catnip for renaissance types.

Theme Two

NEOD participants were motivated by mastery of complex, high risk activities that provided a sense of *flow*. Participant interviews in this section overlap slightly with other sections, but capture the often ephemeral connection of NEOD to their descriptions of flow:

(*Clam*) I was a bored out of my mind as a Navy Fleet aircraft mechanic. I saw a recruiting advertisement for EOD that said it was a challenge, got to work out, jump dive shoot, play with explosives, like what wasn't to like. I was already dying a little every day working on aircraft. Then once I got into the EOD game it was like whoa, this is more fun than anything I ever experienced, I mean the rush from beating an IED is like nothing else. The skills we gain in adventure type sports is wickedly cool and most of our guys would spend money to do this stuff, but they are paying me to do stuff that is just plain fun. Its like time and space just stop when you are *in the zone* (slang: EOD flow). I have some administrative role at the moment and I find myself daydreaming about being back at the show, *in the zone*, trying to find a way to get back to operational stuff.

(*X13*) Team input during crisis is extraordinarily fulfilling, like its hard to articulate. When you are doing something immensely important, working together to make it happen, and know if it goes wrong, the party will be over (slang: death), it's a feeling of pure joy. Beating a device against all odds by throwing some crazy plan together in a short period of time is a high you can't beat.

(*Juggernaut*) this is going to sound really silly, it's a bit embarrassing, but if you really want to know, I got giddy every time I watched a bogus action film as a kid. Each time they used explosives, I just lost it. I mean, I have always been fascinated by explosives. So I steered my childhood towards the goal of being an EOD guy, then I finally get into the game and they let me parachute, dive and shoot. Its like a fantasy life. The feeling I get from doing high pressure work in lousy situations is addicting. Stopping an IED and seeing people that could have died walk away smiling, it sticks with you. That feeling of being stoked, stays with me. I just love this (expletive).

(*X15*) We just do lots of cool stuff, diving, jumping, and demo across the globe. Every day something new. Impact. Saving lives. Then it's the crazy feeling you get when you *do the deed* (slang: live EOD response inferred), there is just nothing like it, it's a high that beats all others when you win in an intense atmosphere, using all kinds of tech, save some citizens. Its like time stops, the heavens part and its what I was meant to do.

(*P4Product*) I dig the variety of people, diversity of work, different locations and cultures. The travel is awesome and having influence on people's lives is fulfilling. But what really acts as my catnip is winning in a high pressure environment. Overcoming evil with a team of rogue nerds just gives me such a rush that I worry about what happens when I get too old to do this anymore. I am not sure I want to give up this level of satisfaction. When I am in the zone with my team getting at a crisis, coming up with crazy solutions and beating terrorists, its just the best feeling. (*X9*) The diversity of technology and excitement hooked me. In the last 6 months I have gone through three countries jumping, diving and doing IED exploitation, we just have an amazing range of opportunities that expand your mind. I exploited an IED previously used by a bad guy and figuring out the components so the next time we see it; we know what we have in order to save lives. What a rush, makes me stoked to think about it, it was a short event that felt like hours.

Theme Three

Autonomy was a universal motivational component for NEOD participants interviewed. NEOD participants in this study universally (22 of 22) insisted upon autonomy as both a motivational force, and a facet of their ability to innovate:

(*Clam*) In NEOD, we are given huge amounts of freedom so we can innovate and scheme, study areas we are interested in, set our own schedule and plan. It's the reverse in staff work, we are painted into artificial boxes with a system that is so jammed up you can't barely win. In NEOD, you have to be completely out of the box in order to achieve the results necessary. When I first talked to an NEOD guy before entering the community, he just did not give a shit about anything other than getting the job done and that was really appealing. NEOD seemed like some kind of Silicon Valley start up for X gamers (slang: professional extreme sport). I wanted an unscripted life and liked the idea of challenging myself.

(X10) I love the freedom to choose what I want to do day to day to get at problems, lots of exciting activities. Chance to save lives. Diving, parachuting shooting, demolition, robots, computers, no need to sit at desk, everything is applied towards the goal of defeating a device. The freedom and autonomy keep us creative. I could not do this if we had the typical constrained environment found in most military organizations. I find it really oppressive to have silly admin tasks to perform and rigid of interacting lock step. Looks like some sort of Google office space out here, but when you need a creative solution, we can make it happen.

(*X11*) We have more freedom from almost every angle you might consider, compared to other parts of the military. Freedom in life helps free thinking develop. Never doing the same thing over and over helps us stay outside the box. We are in a position to ask questions and make stuff happen. We make logical decisions and use our brains to think. This is a thinking mans game. It is probably why we sometimes are viewed sort of unmanageable by the spit and polish types.

(*X14*) Autonomy is awesome and huge motivator in this job. Lack of autonomy crushes team spirit and creativity, because we have skin in the game. We fail and it's pink mist, this is not the time for management good idea fairies to land. We are intelligent, well trained guys with mad team cohesion. Let us work, we will win. We have to be free to create. Letting silly rules interfere with our operations only forces guys out of this structure to work in civilian jobs where they are freed to be creative.

(*P4Product*) As the Master blaster, I just tell the lads the desired outcome and they will get there through networking and experimenting. It's best to let these cats run and sort out their own way. My job is to let them try anything as long as it's safe, but protect them as QC (slang: quality control for safety). It's the Chief's job to protect the guys so they can *get at it*. We need to give them time off to pursue all sorts of stuff so they are versatile. As long as they are working to make something better, actually working to make everything they touch better, we will continue to succeed. These are not guys you develop in some lock step structure. Every interference on their freedom from some administrative requirement tends to reduce creativity, and most importantly, their effectiveness to save lives.

(*X20*) Autonomy breeds innovation and allows you to think outside the the box. The unscripted nature of our job requires loose management. You are a product of your environment, how we develop guys is providing tasks without instructions so we can develop innovation. As the Master Blaster, I rarely tell my guys how to do something. They need to figure that out. I sort of lay back and change their direction if things are looking unsafe. Team expectations are high and we are confident. We expect our team to be the best and will put in the time to make it happen. Another key job of the Master Blaster is to block silly administrative requirements from management. Once management curtails team fluidity, we will lose capability.

(X13) We have an immense amount of freedom compared to almost all other jobs in the military world, because every EOD problem is unique. In the regular military structure, where most of us have done penance, every aspect of a person's life is controlled, and it works well because the regular military responds to problems that can usually be anticipated. But EOD problems are always unique and bad guys are always upgrading to the latest technologies or new innovation. The big military can be slow, but EOD guys with time off will pursue crazy technology interests and gain the fluidity of thought necessary to win. To be creative, you have to live creatively.

(*Odin*) We have immense freedom when compared with almost any industry. NEOD guys have less structure so we can have leeway to innovate. We start later in the day so we can work out in the morning and we make our own schedule based upon needs. We are more oriented towards outcome than a fixed schedule. This helps us perform on the fly (slang: short notice), because we live on the fly (slang: unscripted life) with deliberate practice when we need it to achieve a specific objective. While we have a lot of autonomy, when its time to work, we are held to high performance standards involving life and death. With that in mind, these guys don't turn into couch potatoes when you cut them loose, they are gaining new skills to put in their skill bank for use when needed. Take away the autonomy, and these guys would not be effective and would probably quit.

(*Juggernaut*) We have way more autonomy than others, we are the Google of the military, a bunch of athletic nerd, free range chickens. You can't innovate in a box. You don't go through a (expletive) busting two-year pipeline of eating dirt, then make multiple combat deployments, only to come home

and have your haircut managed. *If we are gonna think free,*
we gotta live free. Don't worry, we are committed, we have
skin in the game. The guys that make up silly rules generally
live a great distance from danger. A good haircut hasn't beat
an IED yet.

Theme Four

NEOD participants are motivated by working in small elite
teams composed of eclectic individuals sharing a common goal.

(*X20*) NEOD people are cool in a nerdy way. It's a
motivated, clever and intelligent community. I'll tell ya what
makes a NEOD guy from my perspective. He fizzled out in
college because there was too much structure. He, or she, I
could care less about gender, is smart. Then something pisses
them off enough to seek out what their life means, and they
find this game. They find a brotherhood of purpose with
athletic intelligent war fighters. Its high risk and low external
reward, but it appeals to humble people with the adventure
bug. From a combat experience perspective, its cool, and *we*
take glory in no glory. NEOD is rewarded by being in high
demand across all military services. But the thing that keeps

you in this game is the connection to team mates. We do so much high speed stuff that no one will ever know about, only other NEOD guys, and that creates this amazing bond. I am bonded in a way with my team mates that simply cannot be replicated elsewhere.

(*X9*) Always wanted to serve, was leaving a small group of guys that worked well together wanted something meaningful with small group atmosphere. I met a NEOD tech before joining the Navy, and 45 minutes after talking to this guy, I knew becoming a frogman was not the career I sought.

(*X14*) I really connect with 30% of our guys, and that 30% sustains my desire to stay connected to the community. Its fulfilling to innovate and very gratifying to solve deadly problems, its immediate and immense. This is winning big. I love working in a small, elite team.

(*Odin*) I started out as a lifeguard as a kid and liked aspect of saving people, but there was not enough action. After college, was looking for something altruistic, small team, engineering related, and exciting. NEOD fit the mold with saving lives, jumping, diving, blowing stuff up, and shooting. But what sold me on it was the people. Once I was exposed to NEOD guys, I just fit the profile, we have a shared purpose. I really like working in small teams of guys I trust that are focused on results.

(*Honeybear*) I like the comradery of small team work and being with guys you can trust.

(*Clam*) I wanted the challenge and the prestige, to work in a small team, with people I could trust.

(*X13*) I wanted to work in a small group with guys I could trust with my life. It has been a chance to be creative, work out, and gain a lot of new technical skills. NEOD is impactful and morally cool.

Research Question Three Summary

All NEOD participants (22 of 22) were strongly motivated by a self-identified sense of purpose. A large number of NEOD participants (20 of 22) were motivated by mastery of complex, high risk activities that provided a sense of *flow*. Autonomy was a universal motivational component for NEOD participants (22 of 22).

NEOD participants were motivated by working in small elite teams composed of eclectic individuals sharing a desire to defeat explosive hazards and save lives.

Summary of Chapter Four

Chapter Four presented findings on how NEOD technicians experience their role in bomb disposal innovation, what motivates them, and how they make decisions. Research questions were designed to investigate the lived experiences of NEOD technicians. The lived experiences of NEOD technicians supported the development of 13 themes generated from the essence of 22 interviews and 3 research questions:

Research Question One: To what extent do NEOD technicians innovate with new techniques during an EOD crisis response?

- Every EOD response is unique.

- Unique EOD responses require time critical innovation that includes networking, questioning, observing, experimenting, and connectional intelligence.

- Crisis innovation is a component of NEOD mindset and taught in the NEOD community.

- NEOD technicians reported egalitarian teams with broad diversity in rank, experience and interests help them succeed.

- NEOD technicians reported exceptional levels of confidence individually and in teams.

Research Question Two: To what extent do NEOD technicians use *rules of thumb* when responding to a crisis?

- NEOD participants were extremely focused on defeating explosive devices and saving lives, but articulated heuristics that emphasized avoidance of rigid structural protocols and standardization of activities.

- NEOD technician's relationship to their high value equipment is intense.

- NEOD decision-making is linear in early portion of their career, but as they gain experience, it becomes more intuitive.

- NEOD participants used heuristics to synthesize complex operational and technical concepts.

Research Question Three: What motivates NEOD technicians to perform their exceptionally dangerous role?

- NEOD participants were strongly motivated by a self-identified sense of purpose.

- NEOD participants were motivated by mastery of complex, high risk activities that provided a sense of *flow*.

- Autonomy was a universal motivational component for NEOD participants interviewed.

- NEOD participants are motivated by working in small elite teams composed of

  eclectic individuals sharing a common goal.

Chapter Five will blend the lived experiences of NEOD technicians with literature findings and bomb disposal practitioner implications. Bomb disposal selection and training implications will also be considered. Broader consideration of potential transferability of crisis innovation techniques for use in business and industry will

be reviewed. Chapter Five will outline future research possibilities.

CHAPTER FIVE: DISCUSSION

This phenomenological study explored how NEOD technicians understand and experience their mindset through the lens of motivation, innovation, and decision-making. Study results offer insight for: (a) researchers, (b) personnel involved in the selection, recruiting and retention bomb disposal technicians, (c) personnel involved with training of bomb disposal technicians and, (d) commercial industries seeking expedited innovation timelines. The NEOD lived experiences of 13 individuals and two teams ($n = 5$, $n = 4$) were captured in face to face interviews on the island of Guam. The NEOD participants lived experiences were categorized into 28 initial cluster groups, and ultimately distilled into 13 primary themes. This chapter blends findings and literature, discusses implications, and justifies further research.

Connection to Literature

Chapter Two presented literature that provided a framework for this study involving the NEOD mindset. Research spanning bomb disposal, motivation, innovation and decision-making offered context for the lived experience of NEOD technicians. Relevant literature helped develop meaning about themes detailed in the study. Previous research had not investigated how NEOD technicians innovated in crisis, what motivated them to perform this role, or how they made decisions. Parallels between published literature and qualitative findings from this study inform relative implications across the fields of innovation, motivation, and decision making.

Innovation

Five themes were identified within the innovation cluster: (a) every EOD response is unique, (b) NEOD crisis innovation included networking, questioning, observing, experimenting, and connectional intelligence, (c) crisis innovation is a component of NEOD mindset and is taught in the NEOD community, (d) diverse egalitarian teams succeed, and (e) NEOD technicians report exceptional confidence. The aforementioned themes parallel extant literature on innovation as difficult to define and ephemeral in nature (Crosson and Apaydin, 2009; Lopes, Kissimoto, Salerno, Carvalho, and Laurindo; 2016). Fagerberg's (2003) research identifying industry specific methods and outcomes of innovation is supported by this study. NEOD participants have a unique world view, or *mindset,* when confronting challenges. The NEOD constellation of innovation themes both supports and expands understanding of the innovation process, particularly in relation to *crisis innovation.*

The first theme in this study is an unusual statement of the NEOD lived experience, and reported by all study participants: **every EOD response is unique**. NEOD participants used this phrase, on average, 6 times during each interview. The statement is sublime, and the implications support the 4 P's of innovation: (a) person, (b) product, (c) process, and (d) press. *Press,* used by Cropley and Cropley (2015) and Cropley (2015, 2010), is the social context and pressure that engenders innovation. Because *every EOD response is unique* is accepted within the NEOD social context, a unique, or innovative response is warranted. Innovation is inherent within acceptance of this unusual reality. Unique solutions to unique problems were accepted as a way of being for NEOD technicians because innovation "consists of a new combination of existing ideas, capabilities, skills, and resources" (Sawyer, 1998, p. 7) combined to achieve an outcome.

This study supports Jalonen's (2011) meta-study findings that uncertainty is a major feature of innovation. *Every EOD response is unique* infers clear uncertainty about what the NEOD operator will face when arriving at a crisis and likely fuels innovation.

The second innovation theme noted in this study stated, **NEOD crisis innovation included networking, questioning, observing, experimenting, and connectional intelligence**. Theme two mirrors previously identified innovation research within business and industry that supported the same traits (Cropley, 2006; Dyer, Gregersen, & Christensen, 2011). NEOD participants noted the value of networking as a primary support mechanism to question and observe, particularly in leadership roles (Officer, Chief). Connectional intelligence has also been defined as divergent thinking by Cropley (2006, 2008). NEOD participants reported extensive ability to observe a broad array of variables and connect them in a unique manner to solve problems, thereby overcoming the divergent thinking paradox (Cropley, 2008) of observation without integration of new ideational relationships.

The third theme identified in the innovation category stated, **crisis innovation is a component of NEOD mindset and is taught in the NEOD community**. NEOD participants all identified a mindset peculiar to their role and that this mindset is taught throughout an NEOD technicians career. Theme three findings support Pisanu and Menapace's (2014) supposition that innovation can be taught, as well as Fagerberg's (2003) and von Hippel's, (2013) research that identified *lead users* as far more innovative than scientific or management researchers. Plattner & Leukert (2015) argued the innovation is a problem framing issue and this study supports that premise with the additional perspective that mindset impacts how the problem is framed. Problem framing is taught within NEOD, as reported by participants, but in the context of a comprehensive worldview identified as the NEOD mindset.

Theme four within the innovation category noted, **diverse egalitarian teams succeed**. NEOD participant teams were an amalgamation of a college educated Junior Officer (JO) with limited experience, a senior Non-Commissioned Officer (NCO) Master EOD technician, a few Junior Enlisted (JE) equally divided between Senior EOD and Basic EOD skill levels. NEOD participants were largely multi-lingual and well travelled, with diverse areas of personal and professional expertise. The combined skills of the NEOD teams interviewed were exceedingly dynamic. The NEOD experiential breadth and depth of skills supports research noting the benefit of diversity in innovation (Basadur & Basadur, 2011; Costa-Font, Courbage, & Mina, 2009; Sawyer 2006). Because NEOD participants noted their tendency to focus intensely on specific skill development, they have exceptionally broad *platform skills* (Brusoni & Prencipe, 2009; Cotter, Pretz, & Kaufman, 2016). Platform skills are abilities that can be leveraged to innovate in crisis, and the broader the diversity of skills on a team, the wider the solution set that can be considered. But diversity in experience and platform skills alone are not sufficient because the entire team needs to question, experiment, observe and connect information. NEOD participants universally noted a disregard for rigid military protocols as part of their NEOD mindset. Extensive research identified organizational culture (Neely and Hii, 2014) and structure (Pisanu and Menapace, 2014) as a primary driver of innovation. This study supports both a relaxed organizational and cultural structure as advantageous to NEOD innovators.

The final theme found within the innovation cluster was surprising: **NEOD technicians reported exceptional levels of confidence individually and in teams**. NEOD participants continually noted their belief that they would *beat any device*

because they would *figure it out* as long as they were *with their team.*
The NEOD team's combined knowledge, skill and ability reservoir
was reported as the elixir from which solutions could be drawn, and
if not available, the team networking capability *would find a way.*
Confidence was demonstrated to be a significant component of the
lived experience of success for innovation among NEOD technicians.
As NEOD team Prometheus noted, *if you don't believe there is a*
solution, you can't find it. NEOD negative outcomes can result in
death and it seems likely a complex constellation of underlying
beliefs pertaining to mortality are involved. Business research
regularly uses the term *innovate or die* to provide emphasis on the
importance of innovation (Collis, 2007). NEOD participants were
extremely confident they would innovate because death was an
actual possibility.

Decision-Making

Four themes were identified within the decision-making
cluster: (a) NEOD participants were extremely focused on defeating
explosive devices and saving lives, but articulated heuristics that
emphasized avoidance of rigid structural protocols and
standardization of activities, (b) NEOD technician's relationship to

their high value equipment is intense, (c) NEOD decision-making is linear in early portion of their career, but as they gain experience, it becomes more intuitive, (d) NEOD participants used heuristics to synthesize complex operational and technical concepts. The lived experiences of NEOD technicians largely support current literature in decision-making, but have several interesting caveats based upon the critical role of equipment and the intense desire to *beat the device* and *stay alive*.

The primary theme identified within the decision making structure was based upon frequency of statements by NEOD participants: **NEOD participants were extremely focused on defeating explosive devices and saving lives, but articulated heuristics that emphasized avoidance of rigid structural protocols and standardization of activities.** Capturing the essence of this theme is peculiar. NEOD technicians reported constant focus on the saving lives when responding to an EOD call but considered the greatest threats to be structural when making decisions. Stopping an IED from *functioning as designed* was an over-riding goal, and the heuristic *what can kill me now* was a universal rule of thumb. Yet underlying the obvious survival heuristics was a lite motif involving structure as another enemy. All NEOD participants repeated *you gotta know the rules to break them* and *don't get tunnel vision*. This is similar to Cropley's (2011) research regarding decision-making within an innovative milieu that required the ability to identify constraints. NEOD participants identified their decision-making constraints as (a) survival, (b) structural protocols, and (c) standardization. NEOD participants captured their prioritization methodology using parallel heuristics: (a) *what can kill me now*, (b) *safety is the only rule*, (c) *non-standard is standard*. This perspective is partially supported by Naturalistic Decision-Making (NDM) theory where situational awareness and expertise are used to make the right choice immediately (Huder, 2012; Klein, 2015).

The second theme concerning decision-making by NEOD technician's is based on the NEOD technician's **intense relationship to their high value equipment**. It may seem counter-intuitive to consider an *intense relationship with equipment* as decision-making function, but the interview data was compelling. NEOD participant's attachment to, knowledge of, and impact on decisions based on equipment status was universal. In most reported operational circumstances, participants reported adjusting decisions based upon what equipment was available, functioning properly, and appropriate to the task. *Take care of your equipment* and it will take care of you because you need to *bet your life on it* were common rules of thumb. During interviews NEOD participants were able to recall the equipment they had available, and the operational status of the equipment, from EOD responses more than a decade ago. Knowledge of equipment use is a common platform skill within innovation (Brusoni & Prencipe, 2009; Cotter, Pretz, & Kaufman, 2016), but the research did not include life support equipment skills. NEOD equipment skills may best be termed critical platform skills because a lack thereof could result in death. NEOD decision making depends upon the equipment.

Theme three within the decision-making cluster was: **NEOD decision-making is linear in early portion of their career, but as they gain experience, it becomes more intuitive**. NEOD participants entered the occupation via a lengthy training program that never really ends. NEOD participants mirrored research on System 1 (emotional, intuitive, fast) and System 2 (deliberate, logical, slow) because they entered NEOD using checklists, moving slowly and acting deliberately but later in their careers, with experience, advanced towards to faster, intuitive decisions (Kahneman, 2011; Tversky & Kahneman, 1983, 1975, 1974, 1973, 1972). Interestingly, NEOD technicians with 2-4 years of experience began to report use of rapid internalized flow charts that appear similar to Gigenrenzer's (2014, 2004, 2003, 2002, 1999) *fast and frugal* decision-making process. Master NEOD participants reported highly sophisticated and internalized, fast and frugal checklists driven by heuristics, but with an interesting caveat relating to time. When time was not limited, NEOD technicians prefer to use checklists, or Emergency Response Plans (ERPs) as a quality control mechanism. NEOD participants continually noted the need to *dial it in*, indicating a need to adjust between System 1 and System 2 depending upon situational requirements. System 2 was a desired, but often unlikely option due to time constraints or the urgency of the situation.

Theme four within the decision making cluster was: **NEOD participants used heuristics to synthesize complex operational and technical concepts**. Master EOD participants noted the burden of training, leading, and keeping an EOD team alive. It is a significant responsibility and with changing personnel and varying degrees of expertise, heuristics was a tool they rely on. The Master EOD technician does not have the time to explain every facet of the EOD art, but they can share rules of thumb. Numerous heuristics were identified by participants that are of significant research interest regarding decision-making: (a) *fast is slow, slow is fast*, (b) *slow is smooth, and smooth is fast*, (c) *trust your instincts*, (d) *muddy boots are better than bloody boots*, (e) *what can kill me now*, (f) *you have to know the rules to break them* (g) *non-standard is standard*, (h) *you have to live free to think free*, (i) *make it better*, and (j) *dial it in*. Conceptually, NEOD heuristics parallel recent fast and frugal business rules (Goleman, 2013; Nunes, Miles, Luck, Barbosa, & Lucena, 2015). Many of the NEOD participants reported being alive today (and hundreds of innocents) because of their use of fast and frugal heuristics during crisis response.

Motivation

Four themes were identified within the motivation cluster: (a) NEOD participants were strongly motivated by a self-identified sense of purpose (b) NEOD participants were motivated by mastery of complex, high risk activities that provided a sense of *flow*, (c) Autonomy was a universal motivational component for NEOD participants interviewed (d) NEOD participants were motivated by working in small elite teams composed of eclectic individuals sharing a common goal. Gollwitzer (1999) noted motivation is a "primary cause of behavior" (cited in Smelser & Baltes, 2001, p.10109) and understanding motivation within NEOD could become an important facet of NEOD selection, training, and retention. Most importantly, understanding NEOD motivation could lead to better results. Prior to this study, NEOD motivation was known to exist in strong quantities because of the lengthy and rigorous training (Bundy & Sims, 2007; Hogan & Hogan, 1984) but NEOD motivation details were unarticulated.

The first theme within the motivation cluster was: **NEOD participants were strongly motivated by a self-identified sense of purpose.** Most NEOD participants noted altruism and impact as a driving motivational force with the common phrases, saving lives and getting results.

Purpose as motivation in NEOD participants strongly parallel Pink's (2009) motivational triad of purpose, mastery, and autonomy. NEOD team participants articulated group reinforcement of purpose as a driving force with statements, we save lives or our team leverage others to help save lives. This information supports Fehr and Fischbacher's (2003) finding that altruistic personalities were able to sway groups towards altruistic behaviors.

The second motivational theme was, **NEOD participants were motivated by mastery of complex, high risk activities that provided a sense of** *flow*. NEOD participants reported the sensation of flow when they conducted high risk activities, particularly defeating explosive hazards, parachuting, and diving. As one participant noted, *that feeling I get when I beat a device and save lives is the best...time slows and a sense of joy just overwhelms me.* This data supports flow as motivational research (Wilder, Csikszentmihalyi, & Csikszentmihalyi, 1989). NEOD participants use of flow as a motivator is supported by updates to Maslow's (1943,1970) hierarchy of needs that identified "cognitive priority triggered by proximate inputs" as motivational (Kenrick, Griskevicius, Neuberg, & Schaller, 2010, p. 293). NEOD participants reported robust proximate inputs during high risk activities that positively triggered cognitive priorities (Hardie-Bick & Bonner, 2015). Csikszentmihalyi's (1990) research identifying complex activity mastery as motivational was supported by data from this study. NEOD participants repeatedly noted how they loved to *solve impossible problems* and *combine whacky technologies to win*. Pink (2009) identified mastery as a motivational pillar and NEOD participants universally reported pleasure from operational mastery. The aforementioned data also supports the concept of mindset used by Dweck (2006) when research identified a growth mindset as questioning, working harder, and enjoying complex challenges.

Autonomy was a universal motivational component for NEOD participants interviewed. NEOD participants were strongly attached to an unscripted life, freedom to make their own schedule, and pursue their own interests. A common participant phrase was we are the *Google of the Navy*, and *we have to live free, to think free*. The primary complaints from NEOD participants were that their effectiveness was diluted by burdensome administrative requirements and *cookie cutter approaches*. From the standpoint of eminent psychologist Norman Dixon (1968), military authoritarianism leads to operational incompetence and NEOD participant results appear to support this supposition. All NEOD leadership level participants identified one of their primary roles as *blocking useless constraints* and helping their team *get at it*. NEOD

participants *like to be in charge* and immensely value their freedom

to make death defying choices. NEOD participants parallel Brymer

and Schweitzer's (2013) research that identified six motivational

factors in extreme sport participants, of which three were directly

reported by NEOD participants: (a) freedom from constraints, (b)

freedom as movement, (c) freedom as choice and responsibility (p.

27). Interestingly, this study did not parallel the extreme sport

participant finding by Brymer and Schweitzer's (2013) identifying

freedom as letting go of the need for control. NEOD participants

reported a significant desire to be in control during their lived

experiences and parallels the theory that level of control impacts

motivation (Amabile, Hill, Hennessey, & Tighe, 1994; Amabile,

1994; Pittman, 1987).

NEOD participants were motivated by working in small

elite teams composed of eclectic individuals sharing a common

goal. Sociality and cultural context are major components of

motivation (Petri & Govern, 2013). Cooper's (1982) finding that

EOD technicians prefer things over people was partially validated in

this study. NEOD participants reported much stronger interest in technology and problem solving, they also identified unusually strong in-group human bonding. The participants report general apathy towards out-group, and even within their functioning groups spend much of their time pursing individual pursuits. As numerous participants noted, we look like a herd of cats, but when it hits the fan, we connect and win. NEOD participants reported a desire to work with people they can *trust enough to gamble their life on it*. To trust at that level, NEOD team members need to *bring something to the table* and have skills that provide group synergy. They report a desire to have diverse members on their team with unique skills, but they need to hold one common goal, *beat the device*. This information is supported by social context theory and motivation cognition theory (Amabile, Hill, Hennessey, & Tighe, 1994; Amabile, 1994; Pittman, 1987). NEOD motivation was demonstrated to be multidimensional in this small study.

Implications and Recommendations

The results of this modest (n = 22) study imply an NEOD mindset exists with parallel's

to Dweck's (2006) growth mindset. The NEOD mindset is multidimensional with three primary subsets: (a) motivation, (b) innovation, and (c) decision-making. Within each subset, numerous components have been identified. The NEOD mindset has not previously been captured in research. Using Boyd's Observe, Orient, Decide, and Act Loop (OODA Loop) (as cited in Ford, 2010), this study has initiated a modest start to observation of the NEOD mindset phenomenon. More expansive research is recommended from the NEOD community of approximately 1500 personnel to define beneficial NEOD traits. A comprehensive understanding of the NEOD mindset would offer advantages in selection, training, and retention of personnel. Enhanced selection, training, and retention would likely improve the NEOD force and be transferable to EOD forces across the globe. Specific NEOD mindset implications and recommendations are detailed next.

Innovation Implications and Recommendations

Successful NEOD technicians must innovate because every problem is unique. Innovation on an abbreviated timeline, with death as a possible outcome, is defined as *crisis innovation* by this study. In the results, NEOD crisis innovation was facilitated by: (a) networking, (b) questioning, (c) observing, (d) experimenting, (e) connectional intelligence, (f) diverse team (g) exceptional confidence and, (h) egalitarian team management. A comprehensive

blended qualitative/quantitative study be conducted across the

NEOD enterprise, with significant focus on identification and

development of crisis innovation core skills. Crisis innovation is

taught, and shared within the NEOD community as tribal knowledge

via heuristics.

NEOD technicians also report a lack of an integrated

computer platform to network with other NEOD technicians because

of the sensitive nature of their role. Recommend the Internet be

leveraged to enhance communication via blogs, posts, email and

video uploads. Networking enhancement infrastructure for NEOD

will expand the larger reservoir of NEOD knowledge among a

community of trust. In turn, larger data reach between interested

NEOD members will provide sustainable, competitive innovation

advantage in crisis. Under the current internal NEOD networking

options available, tactical EOD technicians are operating within pods

of excellence.

Decision-making Implications and Recommendations

NEOD decision-making processes begin at EOD School,

learning a broad array of skills and rules. The art of NEOD is complex, and participants reported emphasis on System 2, check list based decision making when they enter the field, and/or have time available during a crisis. As NEOD progresses in their career and gain experience, their ability to make intuitive decisions improves. Rules of thumb were used extensively by NEOD participants to internalize fast and frugal rules to make rapid decisions. This study recommends further research to capture heuristics used across the EOD community, validate the utility, and maintain a database for use by all NEOD members. Most NEOD participants reported learning their rules of thumb from an *old Master Blaster* with decades of experience. While person to person transmission is useful, capture of data, analysis, and dissemination across global EOD forces would accelerate learning. Improved learning should yield better response outcomes, inferring more lives saved.

Motivation Implications and Recommendations

NEOD participants were driven by a strong sense of purpose, primarily saving lives and impact. The remainder of Pink's (2009) motivational triad including purpose, autonomy and mastery were also validated in this study (Gillard, Gillard, & Pratt, 2015; Fragoso,

Holcombe, McCluney, Fisher, McGonagle, & Friebe, 2016).

Interestingly, NEOD participants also had a high need to experience

flow as well as work in small self-directed teams. This research

implies a pentagon structure with the following nodes (in order of

frequency) of motivation requiring further research: (a) purpose, (b)

autonomy, (c) flow, (d) mastery, and (e) small self-directed teams.

An advantage of a qualitative study is the ability to grasp the level of

emotion attached to a particular lived experience. Autonomy was a

topic that elicited fierce attachment by all participants. While

Napoleon and Patton were quoted as using the term "audacity,

audacity, and more audacity," (cited in Carter & Kourdi, 2003, p. 9),

NEOD participants requested autonomy, autonomy, and more

autonomy. As the global IED crisis expands, the need for EOD

technician's will likely continue to increase. Increased military

personnel generally result in increased layers of management, more

structure, and less freedom (Dixon, 1976). This study implies a

hidden ingredient within NEOD built on autonomy and recommends

further research. NEOD success, followed by growth and

standardization appears a valid threat to community efficacy. In their

lived experience, NEOD participants *need to live free to think free.*

169

As this study was being finalized, fascinating new research was published by Zestcott, Lifshin, Helm and Greenberg, (2016) highlighting the impact of death reminders as a motivational force in sport that actually improved performance by 40%. Greenberg and Arndt (2011) postulated terror management theory to understand fear of inevitable death as a motivator. In this NEOD study, death was noted a minimum of three times for each participant. Perhaps the dark and relentless NEOD humor focused on death acts as a motivational force. NEOD future research is recommended using terror management theory.

Conclusion

The global terror crisis continues unabated, with IEDs being the primary weapon used by destabilizing elements and the primary Counter-IED tool being EOD technicians (Laska, 2015; Revill, 2016). Failure to *defeat the device* from 2011-2014 led to 70,196 casualties, with 54,752 being civilians (Action on Armed Violence, 2016). Understanding the multidimensional NEOD mindset can provide a data set of knowledge to enhance EOD selection, training, retention and response execution across the globe. This phenomenological study (n = 22) captured the lived experiences of

NEOD technician's. The NEOD mindset is multidimensional with three primary subsets: (a) motivation, (b) crisis innovation, and (c) decision-making. Within each subset, numerous components were identified. This study offers preliminary observations about the NEOD experience and how it might be transferred across the global EOD enterprise or perhaps business and industry. NEOD is a community of aggressive altruists delivering life saving impact. Further NEOD research is not only warranted, it may be necessary. NEOD technicians ask *what can kill me now*, but people around the world under threat of IED attacks might ask, *who can save me now?*

References

Action on Armed Violence. (2016, April 19). *The impact of explosive weapons.* Retrieved from https://aoav.org.uk/infographic/four-years-of-harm-aoav-records-over-110000-civilian-casualties-of-explosive-violence-2011-2014

Anthony, S. D. (2008). *The innovator's guide to growth: Putting disruptive innovation to work.* Boston, MA: Harvard Business Press.

Amabile, T. M. (1983). The social psychology of creativity: A componential conceptualization. *Journal of Personality and Social Psychology, 45*, 357-376. doi:10.1037/0022-3514.45.2.357

Amabile, T. M., Hill, K. G., Hennessey, B. A., & Tighe, E. M. (1994). The Work Preference inventory: Assessing intrinsic and extrinsic motivational orientations. *Journal of Personality and Social Psychology, 66*, 950-967. doi:10.1037/0022-3514.66.5.950

Applebaum, M. (2012). Phenomenological psychological research as science. *Journal of Phenomenological Psychology, 43*(1), 36-72. doi:10.1163/156916212x632952

Asken, M. J., Christensen, L. W., & Grossman, D. (2010).

Warrior mindset: Mental toughness skills for a nation's defenders: Performance psychology applied to combat. Millstadt, IL: Human Factor Research Group.

Baas, M., De Dreu, C. W., & Nijstad, B. A. (2008). A meta-analysis of 25 years of mood-creativity research: Hedonic tone, activation, or regulatory focus? *Psychologica Bulletin, 134,* 779-806. doi:10.1037/a0012815

Babula, M. W. (2013). The unlikely Samaritans. *Journal of Applied Social Psychology, 43* 899-908. doi:10.1057/9781137031297

Bandura, A. (1985). Model of causality in social learning theory. *Cognition and Psychotherapy,* 81–99. doi:10.1007/978-1-4684-7562-3_3

Bandura, A., & Schunk, D. H. (1981). Cultivating competence, self-efficacy, and intrinsic interest through proximal self-motivation. *Journal of Personality and Social Psychology, 41,* 586–598. doi:10.1037/0022-3514.41.3.586

Banks, L. M. (2013). Working with special operations forces. *Military Psychologists' Desk Reference,* 67–70. doi:10.1093/med:psych/9780199928262.003.0014

Basadur, M., & Basadur, T. (2011). Where are the generators?

Psychology of Aesthetics, Creativity, and the Arts, 5(1), 29-42.

doi:10.1037/a0017757

Baláz, V., Bacová, V., & Skriniar, P. (2014). Experience and

information search patterns in complex decision-making. *Studia*

Psychologica, 56(1), 3-20. doi:10.1002/psp.1858

Barreda-Tarrazona, I., Jaramillo-Gutierrez, A., Navarro-

Martinez, D., & Sabater-Grande, G. (2014). The role of forgone

opportunities in decision-making under risk. *Journal of*

Risk and Uncertainty, 49(2), 167. doi:10.1007/s11166-014-9201-4

Bates, M. J. (2002). A risk factor model predicting the relationship

between stress and performance in Explosive Ordnance Disposal

(EOD) training. *PsycEXTRA Dataset.* doi:10.1037/e431062005-001

Beersma, B., Greer, L. L., Dalenberg, S., & De Dreu, C. W.

(2016). Need for structure as asset and liability in dynamic team

decision-making. *Group Dynamics: Theory, Research, And Practice,*

20(1), 16-33. doi:10.1037/gdn0000037

Benetka, G., & Joerchel, A. C. (2015). Psychology as a

phenomenological science. *Psychology as the Science of Human

Being*, 17–32. doi:10.1007/978-3-319-21094-0_2

Bermudez, P., & Zatorre, R. J. (2009). The absolute pitch mind

continues to reveal itself. *Journal of Biology*, 8(8), 75.

doi:10.1186/jbiol171

Bernhardsdóttir, Á. E. (2015). Decision making and decision-

making unit. *Crisis-Related Decision-Making and the Influence of

Culture on the Behavior of Decision Makers*,57–94.

doi:10.1007/978-3-319-20714-8_5

Berns, G. (2008). *Iconoclast: A neuroscientist reveals how to think

differently*. Boston, MA: Harvard Business School Press.

Bhat, I. A. (2015). Jugaad innovation: A frugal and flexible

approach to innovation for the 21st century. *African Journal of

Science, Technology, Innovation, and Development*,

   7(1), 71–72. doi:10.1080/20421338.2015.1006909

Bhatia, S. (2014). Sequential sampling and paradoxes of risky

choice. *Psychonomic Bulletin & Review, 21*, 1095-1111.

doi:10.3758/s13423-014-0650-1

Bishop, M. A., & Trout, J. D. (2005). *Epistemology and the psychology of human judgment.* New York, NY: Oxford University Press. doi:10.1093/0195162293.001.0001

Birchall, P. (1997). *The longest walk: The world of bomb disposal.* London, UK: Arms andArmour.

Bogdan, R., & Taylor, S. J. (1975). *Introduction to qualitative research methods: A phenomenological approach to the social sciences.* New York, NY: Wiley.

Bolton, M. (2015). From minefields to minespace: An archeology of the changing architecture of autonomous killing in U.S. Army field manuals on landmines, booby traps, and IEDs.*Political Geography, 46,* 41-53. doi:10.1016/j.polgeo.2014.11.002

Borders, J., Polander, N., Klein, G., & Wright, C. (2015). ShadowBox™: Flexible training to impart the expert mindset. *Procedia Manufacturing, 3,* 1574–1579. doi:10.1016/j.promfg.2015.07.444

Brakel, L. A. W. (2013). *The ontology of psychology: Questioning foundations in the philosophy of mind.* New York, NY: Routledge.

Brafman, O., & Beckstrom, R. A. (2006). *The starfish and the spider: The unstoppable power of leaderless organizations.* New York, NY: Portfolio.

Bryant, D. J. (2014). Strategy selection in cue-based decision-making. *Canadian Journal of Experimental Psychology, 68*(2), 97-110. doi:10.1037/cep0000020

Brymer, E., & Schweitzer, R. (2013). The search for freedom in extreme sports: A phenomenological exploration. *Psychology of Sport and Exercise*, 14, 865–873. doi:10.1016/j.psychsport.2013.07.004

Brunell, A. B., & Buelow, M. T. (2015). Narcissism and performance on behavioral decision-making tasks. *Journal of Behavioral Decision-Making.* doi:10.1002/bdm.1900

Brusoni, S., & Prencipe, A. (2009). Design rules for platform leaders. *Platforms, Markets, and Innovation.* doi:10.4337/9781849803311.00020

Budde, R. (1995). The story of Velcro. *Physics World*, 8(1), 22–22. doi:10.1088/2058-7058/8/1/20

Buel, W. D. (1960). The validity of behavioral rating scale items for the assessment of individual creativity. *Journal of Applied*

Psychology, 44, 407-412. doi:10.1037/h0046652

Bukkyō Dendō Kyōkai. (1980). *The teaching of Buddha.* Tokyo,
Japan: Bukkyo Dendo Kyokai.

Bundy, E., & Sims, R. (2007). Commonalities in an uncommon
profession: Bomb disposal. *Proceedings Ascilite Singapore 2007.*
Retrieved from
http://www.ascilite.org/conferences/singapore07/procs/bundy.pdf

Bush, E. K. (2004). *America's first frogman: The Draper Kauffman
story.* Annapolis, MD: Naval Institute Press.

Buss, D. M. (2015). Mating. *The Handbook of Evolutionary
Psychology,* 251–257. doi:10.1002/9780470939376.part3

Buss, D. M., & Schmitt, D. P. (1993). Sexual strategies theory: An
evolutionary perspective   on human mating. *Psychological
Review, 100,* 204–232. doi:10.1037/0033-295x.100.2.204

Butler, J. V., Guiso, L., & Jappelli, T. (2014). The role of intuition
and reasoning in driving aversion to risk and ambiguity. *Theory and
Decision, 77,* 455-484. doi:10.1007/s11238-013-9407-y

Carpenter, S. (2016). *The systems mindset: Managing the
machinery of your life.* Austin, TX: Greenleaf.

Carter, S., & Kourdi, J. (2003). The road to audacity. *The Road to Audacity*, 6–21. doi:10.1057/9780230508798_2

Castela, M., Kellen, D., Erdfelder, E., & Hilbig, B. E. (2014). The impact of subjective recognition experiences on recognition heuristic use: A multinomial processing tree approach. *Psychonomic Bulletin & Review, 21*, 1131-1138. doi:10.3758/s13423-014

Cavojová, V., & Hanák, R. (2014). How much information do you need? Interaction of intuitive processing with expertise. *Studia Psychologica, 56*(2), 83-87. Retrieved from http://search.proquest.com/openview/4661ca7e3b8cef705f557780d1 ba2821/1

Chatterjee, S., Atav, G., Min, J., & Taylor, D. (2014). Choosing the sure gain and the sure loss: Uncertainty avoidance and the reflection effect. *The Journal of Consumer Marketing. 31*, 351-359. doi:10.1108/jcm-04-2014-0949

Chomsky, N. (1980). *Rules and representations*. New York, NY: Columbia University Press.

Christensen, C. M. (1997). *The innovator's dilemma: When new technologies cause great firms to fail*. Boston, MA: Harvard

179

Business School Press.

Christensen, C. M. (2013). *The innovator's solution: Creating and sustaining successful growth.* Boston, MA: Harvard Busines Review Press.

Cimpian, A., & Salomon, E. (2014). Refining and expanding the proposal of an inherence heuristic in human understanding. *Behavioral and Brain Sciences, 37*, 506-527. doi:10.1017/s0140525x14000028

Colaizzi, P. (1978). Psychological research as a phenomenologist views it. In R. Valle & M. King, *Existential-phenomenological alternatives for psychology.* New York, NY: Oxford University Press.

Collis, J. (2007). *Innovate or die: Outside the square business thinking.* Pymble, N. S. W: HarperCollins (Australia).

Conflict Armament Research, (February, 2016). *Tracing the components used in Islamic State IEDs.* Retrieved from http://www.conflictarm.com/wp-content/uploads/2016/02

Cooper, C. L. (1982). Personality characteristics of successful bomb disposal experts. *Journal of Occupational and Environmental Medicine*, 24, 653–655. doi:10.1097/00043764-198209000-0000P

Costa-Font, J., Courbage, C., & Mina, A. (2009). Innovation and health: pathways to new technologies. *Economics of Innovation and New Technology, 18*, 403–406. doi:10.1080/10438590802547092

Cotter, K. N., Pretz, J. E., & Kaufman, J. C. (2016). Applicant extracurricular involvement predicts creativity better than traditional admissions factors. *Psychology of Aesthetics, Creativity, and the Arts, 10*(1), 2-13. doi:10.1037/a0039831

Cox, D., Hallam, R., O'Connor, K., & Rachman, S. (1983). An experimental analysis of fearlessness and courage. *British Journal of Psychology, 74*(1), 107–117.doi:10.1111/j.2044-8295.1983.tb01847.x

Creswell, J. W. (2013). *Qualitative inquiry & research design: Choosing among five approaches.* Los Angeles, CA: Sage.

Cropley, A. (2006). Creativity: A social approach. *Roeper Review, 28*(3), 125–130. doi:10.1080/02783190609554351

Cropley, D. H. (2015). Promoting creativity and innovation in engineering education.

   Psychology of Aesthetics, Creativity, and the Arts, 9, 161-171.

doi:10.1037/aca0000008

Cropley, D., & Cropley, A. J. (2015). *The psychology of innovation in organizations.* doi:10.1017/cbo978131610481

Cropley, D. (2010). *The dark side of creativity.* New York, NY: Cambridge University Press.

Crossan, M. M., & Apaydin, M. (2009). A Multi-Dimensional Framework of Organizational. Innovation: A Systematic Review of the Literature. Journal of Management Studies, 47(6), 1154–1191. doi:10.1111/j.1467-6486.2009.00880.x

Crum, A. J., Salovey, P., & Achor, S. (2013). Rethinking stress: The role of mindsets in determining the stress response. *Journal of Personality and Social Psychology, 104,* 716-733. doi:10.1037/a0031201

Cui, Z. (2015). Decision-making in cross-functional teams: The role of decision power.*Decision Sciences, 47,* 492–523. doi:10.1111/deci.12188

Csikszentmihalyi, M. (1990). *Flow: The psychology of optimal experience.* New York, NY: Harper & Row. doi:10.1037/e597022010-001

Dane, E., Baer, M., Pratt, M. G., & Oldham, G. R. (2011).
Rational versus intuitive problem solving: How thinking 'off the beaten path' can stimulate creativity. *Psychology of Aesthetics, Creativity, and the Arts, 5*, 3-12. doi:10.1037/a0017698

David-Persse, K. K. (2015). Background and advantages of a tiered ems response in a large, fire-based ems model. *Health Care Current Reviews, 03*. doi:10.4172/2375-4273.1000138

Davis, M. H., Hall, J. A., & Mayer, P. S. (2016). Developing a new measure of entrepreneurial mindset: Reliability, validity, and implications for practitioners. *Consulting Psychology Journal: Practice and Research, 68*(1), 21-48. doi:10.1037/cpb0000045

Den Dekker, W. (2013). Global mindset: Theoretical backgrounds. *Global Mindset and Leadership Effectiveness,* 38–63. doi:10.1057/9781137351968_3

Deutsch, D. (2013). Absolute pitch. *The Psychology of Music,* 141–182. doi:10.1016/b978-0-12-381460-9.00005-5

Dolnik, A. (2016). Terrorist innovation. *Combating Transnational Terrorism,* 49–66. doi:10.11610/ctt.ch04

Dixon, N. F. (1976). *On the psychology of military incompetence.* New York, NY: Basic Books.

183

Dowell, J. (2016). Coordination of decision-making in crisis management. *Fusion Methodologies in Crisis Management*, 489–499. doi:10.1007/978-3-319-22527-2_23

Draper, S. R., & Naval Postgraduate School, Monterey, CA (2006). *EOD, up!": How explosive ordnance disposal forces can best support operations forces*. Ft. Belvoir, ST: Defense Technical Information Center.

Drechsler, M., Katsikopoulos, K., & Gigerenzer, G. (2014). Axiomatizing bounded rationality: The priority heuristic. *Theory and Decision, 77*(2), 183-196. doi:10.1007/s11238-013-9393-0

Dreier, A. S. (2012). *Strategy, planning & litigating to win: Orchestrating trial outcomes with systems theory, psychology, military science, and utility theory*. Boston, MA: Conatus Press.

Dubreuil, L. (2009). Dexter Filkins, the forever war. *Oxford Literary Review, 31*, 262–266. doi:10.3366/e030514980900056x

Duckworth, A. (2016). *Grit: The power of passion and perseverance*. New York, NY: Scribner.

Duckworth, A. L., Peterson, C., Matthews, M. D., & Kelly, D. R. (2007). Grit: Perseverance and passion for long-term goals. *Journal of Personality and Social Psychology*, 92(6), 1087–1101.

doi:10.1037/0022-3514.92.6.1087

Durham, J. F., & Hay, D. (2003). *You only blow yourself up once: Confessions of a World War Two bomb disposaleer*. New York, NY: iUniverse.

Dweck, C. S. (2015). The remarkable reach of growth mind-sets. *Sci Am Mind*, 27(1), 36–41. doi:10.1038/scientificamericanmind0116-36

Dweck, C. S. (2006). *Mindset: The new psychology of success*. New York, NY:Random House.

Dyer, J., Gregersen, H. B., & Christensen, C. M. (2011). *The innovator's DNA: Mastering the five skills of disruptive innovators*. Boston, MA: Harvard Business Press.

Eidson, E. & Martinez, V. (2015, March 12). Personal interview at *Future Threats Working Group*, Stump Neck, MD.

Engelmann, J. B., & Pessoa, L. (2014). Motivation sharpens exogenous spatial attention. *Motivation Science*, *1*(S), 64-72. doi:10.1037/2333-8113.1.S.64

Englander, M. (2012). The interview: Data collection in descriptive phenomenological human scientific research. *Journal of Phenomenological Psychology*, 43, 13–35.

doi:10.1163/156916212x632943

Epstein, A. N. (1982). Instinct and motivation as explanations for complex behavior. *The Physiological Mechanisms of Motivation,* 25–58. doi:10.1007/978-1-4612-5692-2_2

Ericsson, K. A. (2016). *Peak: Secrets from the new science of expertise.* Boston, MA: Mifflin Harcourt.

Fagerberg, J., Mowery, D. C., & Nelson, R. R. (2005). *The Oxford handbook of innovation.* Oxford, England: Oxford UniversityPress.

Fehr, E., & Fischbacher, U. (2003). The nature of human altruism. *Nature, 425*(6960), 785–791.doi:10.1038/nature02043

Finlay, L. (2014). Engaging phenomenological analysis. *Qualitative Research in Psych*ology,

11(2), 121–141. doi:10.1080/14780887.2013.807899

Fitzpatrick, J. (2003). Speaking law to power: The war against terrorism and human rights. *European Journal of International Law, 14*(2), 241–264. doi:10.1093/ejil/14.2.241

Ford, D. (2010). *A vision so noble: John Boyd, the OODA Loop, and America's War on Terror.* Durham, NH: Warbird Books.

Forgeard, M. C., & Mecklenburg, A. C. (2013). The two dimensions of motivation and a reciprocal model of the creative process. *Review Of General Psychology, 17*(3), 255-266.

doi:10.1037/a0032104

Fowinkel, T. (2014). *Human resource management systems in new*

business creation. doi:10.1007/978-3-658-05982-8

Fragoso, Z. L., Holcombe, K. J., McCluney, C. L., Fisher, G. G.,

McGonagle, A. K., & Friebe, S.J. (2016). Burnout and

Engagement Relative Importance of Predictors and Outcomes in

Two Health Care Worker Samples. *Workplace Health & Safety,*

2165079916653414. doi:10.1037/e567712014-001

Frank, A. (2015, May 26). NCT explosive Asia 2015: C-IED and

EOD in a challenging environment. Retrieved from

http://www.cbrneportal.com

Frankl, V. E. (2006). *Man's search for meaning.* Boston, MA:

Beacon Press.

Gaubinger, K., Rabl, M., Swan, S., & Werani, T. (2014). Idea

management and open innovation. *Innovation and Product*

Management, 83–113. doi:10.1007/978-3-642-54376-0_5

Gigerenzer, G. (1999). *Simple heuristics that make us smart.* New

York, NY: Oxford University Press.

Gigerenzer, G. (2002). *Bounded rationality: The adaptive toolbox.* Cambridge, MA: MIT

Press.

Gigerenzer, G. (2003). *Calculated risks: How to know when numbers deceive you.* NewYork, NY: Simon and Schuster.

Gigerenzer, G. (2004). Mindless statistics. *Journal of Socio-Economics, 33,* 587–606. doi:10.1016/j.socec.2004.09.033

Gigerenzer, G. (2007). *Gut feelings: The intelligence of the unconscious.* New York, NY: Viking Press.

Gigerenzer, G. (2014). *Risk savvy: How to make good decisions.* New York, NY: Viking Press.

Gigerenzer, G., & Edwards, A. G. K. (2003). Simple tools for understanding risks: from innumeracy to insight. *British Medical Journal, 327,* 741–744. doi:10.1136/bmj.327.7417.741

Gigerenzer, G., & Hoffrage, U. (1995). How to improve Bayesian reasoning without instruction: Frequency formats. *Psychological Review, 102,* 684–704. doi:10.1037/0033-295X.102.4.684

Gigerenzer, G., & Hoffrage, U. (1999). Overcoming difficulties in Bayesian reasoning: A reply to Lewis & Keren and Mellers &

McGraw. *Psychological Review, 106,* 425–430. doi:10.1037/0033-295X.106.2.425

Gigerenzer, G., & Muir Gray, J. A. (Eds.). (2011). *Better doctors, better patients, better decisions: Envisioning health care 2020.* Cambridge, MA: MIT Press.

Gigerenzer, G., & Murray, D. J. (1987). *Cognition as intuitive statistics.* Hillsdale, NJ: Erlbaum.

Gigerenzer, G., Fiedler, K., & Olsson, H. (2012). Rethinking cognitive biases as environmental consequences. In P. M. Todd, G. Gigerenzer, & the ABC Research Group. Ecological *Rationality: Intelligence in the world* (pp. 80–110). New York, NY:Oxford University Press.

Gigerenzer, G., Gaissmaier, W., Kurz-Milcke, E., Schwartz, L. M., & Woloshin, S. (2007). Helping doctors and patients make sense of health statistics. *Psychological Science in the Public Interest, 8,* 53–96. doi:10.1111/j.1539-6053.2008.00033.x

Gigerenzer, G., Hertwig, R., & Pachur, T. (Eds.). (2011). *Heuristics: The foundations of adaptive behavior.* New York, NY: Oxford University Press.

Gigerenzer, G., Hoffrage, U., & Kleinbölting, H. (1991).
Probabilistic mental models: A Brunswikian theory of confidence.
Psychological Review, 98, 506–528. doi:10.1037/0033-
295X.98.4.506

**Gigerenzer, G., Swijtink, Z., Porter, T., Daston, L., Beatty, J., &
Krüger, L. (1989).** *The empire of chance: How probability changed
science and everyday life.* Cambridge, UK: Cambridge University
Press.

Gillard, S., Gillard, S., & Pratt, D. (2015). A pedagological study
of intrinsic motivation in the classroom through autonomy, mastery,
and purpose. *Contemporary Issues in Education Research, 8*, 1.
doi:10.19030/cier.v8i1.9045

Giorgi, A. (1997). The theory, practice, and evaluation of the
phenomenological method as a qualitative research procedure.
Journal of Phenomenological Psychology, 28(2), 235–260.
doi:10.1163/156916297x00103

Giorgi, A. (1992). Description versus interpretation: Competing
alternative strategies for qualitative research. *Journal of*

Phenomenological Psychology, *23*(2), 119–135.

doi:10.1163/156916292x00090

Goleman, D. (2011). *Leadership: The power of emotional intelligence: Selected writings.* Northampton, MA: More Than Sound.

Goleman, D. (2013). *Focus: The hidden driver of excellence.* New York, NY: HarperCollins.

Glicksohn, J., & Bozna, M. (2000). Developing a personality profile of the bomb-disposal expert: The role of sensation seeking and field dependence–independence. *Personality and Individual Differences*, *28*(1), 85–92.

doi:10.1016/s0191-8869(99)00083-5

Goleman, D., Boyatzis, R. E., & McKee, A. (2002). *Primal leadership: Realizing the power of emotional intelligence.* Boston, MA: Harvard Business School Press.

Gollwitzer, P. (1986). Action phases and mind-sets. In E. T. Higgins & E. M. Sorrentino (Eds.), *Handbook of motivation and cognition: Foundations of social behavior.* (526-546) New York, NY: Guilford Press.

Good, C., Rattan, A., & Dweck, C. S. (2012). Why do women opt out? Sense of belonging and women's representation in mathematics. *Journal of personality and social psychology, 102*(4), 700. doi: 101016/201112012

Goodman, M. (2015). *Future crimes everything is connected, everyone is vulnerable and what we can do about it.* New York, NY: Doubleday.

Greenberg, J., & Arndt, J. (2011). Terror management theory. *Handbook of theories of social psychology, 1,* 398-415. doi:10.4135/9781446249215.n20

Gurney, P. (1993). *Braver men walk away.* London, UK: Harper Collins.

Hardie-Bick, J., & Bonner, P. (2015). Experiencing flow, enjoyment, and risk in skydiving and climbing. *Ethnography, 17,* 369-387. doi:10.1177/1466138115609377

Harris, D. J., & Reiter-Palmon, R. (2015). Fast and furious: The influence of implicit aggression, premeditation, and provoking situations on malevolent creativity. *Psychology of Aesthetics, Creativity, and the Arts, 9*(1), 54-64. doi:10.1037/a0038499

Helson, R., & Srivastava, S. (2001). Three paths of adult development: Conservers, seekers, and achievers. *Journal of Personality And Social Psychology, 80,* 995-1010. doi:10.1037/0022-3514.80.6.995

Herzberger, S. D., & Dweck, C. S. (1978). Attraction and delay of gratification. *Journal of Personality,* 46(2), 215–227. doi:10.1111/j.1467-6494.1978.tb00176.x

Hogan, J., & Hogan, R. (1989). Noncognitive predictors of performance during explosive ordnance disposal training. *Military Psychology, 1*(3), 117.doi:10.1207/s15327876mp0103_1

Hogan, J., & Holland, B. (2003). Using theory to evaluate personality and job-performance relations: A socioanalytic perspective. *Journal of Applied Psychology, 88*(1), 100-112. doi:10.1037/0021-9010.88.1.100

Holland, J. L. (1968). Test reviews. *Journal of Counseling Psychology, 15*(3), 297-298. doi:10.1037/h0025735

Huder, R. C. (2012). *Crisis decision-making, in disaster operations and decision-making.* Hoboken, NJ: Wiley & Sons. doi: 10.1002/9781118178539.ch2

Husserl, E. (1970). *Logical investigations*. London, UK: Routledge and K. Paul. Huta, V. (2016). Meaning as a subjective experience. *Journal of Constructivist Psychology*, 1–6. doi:10.1080/10720537.2015.1119088

Jalonen, H. (2011). The uncertainty of innovation: A systematic review of the literature. *Journal of Management Research*, 4(1). doi:10.5296/jmr.v4i1.1039

Jappy, M. J. (2001). *Danger UXB: The remarkable story of the disposal of unexploded bombs during the Second World War.* London, UK: Channel 4 Books.

Jerard, J., & Mohamed Nasir, S. (2015). Resilience and resolve: Community engagement to community resilience. *Communities Against Terrorism*, 1–15. doi:10.1142/9781783267743_0001

Jonason, P. K., Richardson, E. N., & Potter, L. (2015). Self-reported creative ability and the Dark Triad traits: An exploratory study. *Psychology of Aesthetics, Creativity, and the Arts*, 9, 488-494. doi:10.1037/aca0000037

Kahneman, D., & Tversky, A. (1972). Subjective probability: A judgment of representativeness. *Cognitive Psychology*, 3, 430 454. doi: 10.1016/00010-0285(72)90016-3

Kahneman, D. (2011). *Thinking fast and slow*. New York, NY: Farrar, Straus, and Giroux.

Katagiri, N. (2014). *Adapting to win: How insurgents fight and defeat foreign states*. Boston, MA: University of Pennsylvania Press. doi:10.9783/9780812290134

Kaushik, R., & Saha, S. (2016). *Armed forces and insurgents in modern Asia*. London, UK: Routledge. doi:10.4324/9781315625416

Kenrick, D. T., Griskevicius, V., Neuberg, S. L., & Schaller, M. (2010). Renovating the pyramid of needs: Contemporary extensions built upon ancient foundations. *Perspectives on Psychological Science, 5*, 292–314. doi:10.1177/1745691610369469

Klein, G. (2015). A naturalistic decision-making perspective on studying intuitive decision-making. *Journal of Applied Research in Memory and Cognition, 4*(3), 164–168. doi:10.1016/j.jarmac.2015.07.001

Klein, G. (2008). Naturalistic decision-making. *Human Factors: The Journal of the Human Factors and Ergonomics Society, 50*, 456–460. doi:10.1518/001872008x288385

Kluch, S. P., & Vaux, A. (2016). The on-random nature of

terrorism: An exploration of where and how global trends of

terrorism have developed over 40 years. *Studies in*

Conflict & Terrorism. doi:10.1080/1057610x.2016.1159070

Kim, K. H. (2011). The APA 2009 Division 10 debate: Are the

Torrance tests of creative thinking still relevant in the 21st century?

Psychology of Aesthetics, Creativity, and the Arts, 5, 302-308.

doi:10.1037/a0021917

Knoke, D., & Yang, S. (2008). Social Network Analysis.
doi:10.4135/9781412985864

Kotler, S. (2014). *The rise of superman: Decoding the science of*

ultimate human performance. Boston, MA: Harvest.

Kruger, D. J., Wang, X. T., & Wilke, A. (2007). Towards the

development of an evolutionarily valid domain-specific risk-taking

scale. *Evolutionary Psychology, 5*.

doi:10.1177/147470490700500306

Kumar, T. (2015). Rational mind and heuristics in medical

diagnostic decision-making. *British Journal of Medicine and*

Medical Research, 8, 82–87. doi:10.9734/bjmmr/2015/16530

LaFree, G., Dugan, L., & Miller, E. (2015). *Putting terrorism in context: Lessons from the global terrorism database*. London, UK: Routledge.

Lao, Z. & Lau, D. C. (1963). *Tao te ching*. Baltimore, MD: Penguin Books.

Langley, P., Pearce, C., Barley, M., & Emery, M. (2014). Bounded rationality in problem solving: Guiding search with domain-independent heuristics. *Mind & Society, 13*, 83-95. doi: 10.1007/s11299-014-0143-y

Laska, P. R. (2015). *Bombs, IEDs, and explosives: Identification, investigation, and disposal techniques*. Boca Raton, FL: CRC Press.

Leatherwood, J. M. (2012). *Nine from Aberdeen*. Newcastle upon Tyne, UK: Cambridge Scholars Publishing.

Lewicka, D. (2010). The impact of HRM on creating pro-innovative work environment.International Journal of Innovation and Learning, 7(4), 430. doi:10.1504/ijil.2010.032932

Lintern, G. (2010). A comparison of the decision ladder and the recognition-primed decision model. *Journal of Cognitive Engineering and Decision Making, 4*, 304–327. doi:10.1177/155534341000400404

Lipshitz, R., Klein, G., Orasanu, J., & Salas, E. (2001). Taking stock of naturalistic decision making. *Journal of Behavioral Decision Making, 14*, 331–352. doi:10.1002/bdm.381

Lopes, A. P. V. B. V., Kissimoto, K. O., Salerno, M. S., Carvalho, M. M. de, & Laurindo, F. J. B. (2016). Innovation management: A systematic literature analysis of the innovation management evolution. *Brazilian Journal of Operations & Production Management., 13*, 16. doi:10.14488/bjopm.2016.v13.n1.a2

Lucio, M. (2015, December 1). *Zeropoint CEO Perry Sasnett featured in the red bulletin.* Retrieved from http://www.zeropointusa.com/blog/zero-point-ceo-perry-sasnett featured-in-the-red-bulletin

Lyytinen, K. (2016). Unrelenting innovation: How to build a culture for market dominance by Gerard J. Tellis (San Francisco, CA: Jossey-Bass, 2013), *Design Issues, 32*, 114–116. doi:10.1162/desi_r_00405

Malmo, R. B. (1959). Physiological indicants of motivation and of "Arousal." *Acta Psychologica, 15,* 221–222. doi:10.1016/s0001-6918(59)80093-7

Man, J. (2013). *Ninja: 1,000 years of the shadow warrior*. New York, NY: William Morrow.

Manitoba Network for Science & Technology. (1990). *MindSet*. Winnipeg, Canada: Manitoba Network for Science & Technology.

Maslow, A. H. (1943). A theory of human motivation. *Psychological Review, 50*, 370–396. doi:10.1037/h0054346

Maslow, A. H. (1970). *Motivation and personality*. New York, NY: Harper & Row.

Mastrogiorgio, A., & Petracca, E. (2014). Numerals as triggers of system 1 and system 2 in the 'bat and ball' problem. *Mind & Society, 13*(1), 135-148. doi: 10.1007/s11299-014-0138-8

Maul, A. (2013). On the ontology of psychological attributes. *Theory & Psychology, 23*, 752–769.doi:10.1177/0959354313506273

McChrystal, S. A. (2013). *My share of the task: A memoir*. New York: Portfolio/Penguin.

McChrystal, S. A., Collins, T., Silverman, D., & Fussell, C. (2015). *Team of teams: New rules of engagement for a complex world*. New York, NY: Portfolio / Penguin.

McCullar, S. (2013). Decision-making. In K. B. Penuel, M. Statler, & R. Hagen (Eds.), *Encyclopedia of crisis management* (Vol. 2, pp.

245-246). Thousand Oaks, CA: SAGE Publications Ltd.

doi:10.4135/9781452275956.n84

McWilliams, S. A. (2015). Cultivating constructivism: Inspiring

intuition and promoting process and pragmatism. *Journal of*

Constructivist Psychology, *29*, 1–29.

doi:10.1080/10720537.2014.980871

Meadows, D. H., & Wright, D. (2008). *Thinking in systems: A*

primer. White River Junction, VT: Chelsea Green Pub.

Merriam, S. B. (2002). *Qualitative research in practice: Examples*

for discussion and analysis.San Francisco, CA: Jossey-Bass.

Michalkiewicz, M., & Erdfelder, E. (2016). Individual differences

in use of the recognition heuristic are stable across time, choice

objects, domains, and presentation formats.*Memory & Cognition, 44*,

454-468. doi:10.3758/s13421-015-0567-6

Michell, J. (2004). The place of qualitative research in psychology.

Qualitative Research in Psychology, *1*, 307–319.

doi:10.1191/1478088704qp020oa

Monasterio, E. (2012). Personality characteristics in extreme sports

athletes: Morbidity and mortality in mountaineering and BASE

jumping. *Adventure and Extreme Sports Injuries*,

303-314. doi: 10.1007/978-1-4471-4363-5_14

Moustakas, C. (1994). *Phenomenological research methods.*

Thousand Oaks, CA: Sage.

doi:10.4135/9781412995658

Morse, J. M. (2015). Analytic strategies and sample size.

Qualitative Health Research, 25, 1317–1318.

doi:10.1177/1049732315602867

Morse, J. M. (2000). Determining sample size. *Qualitative Health*

Research, 10(1), 3–5. doi:10.1177/104973200129118183

Moulton, J. (2009). Rethinking IED strategies: From Iraq to

Afghanistan. *Military Review, 89*(4), 26. Retrieved from

http://usacac.army.mil/CAC2/MilitaryReview/repository/MilitaryRe

view_200908310001-MD.xml

Mueller, C. M., & Dweck, C. S. (1998). Praise for intelligence can

undermine children's motivation and performance. *Journal of*

personality and social psychology, 75(1), 33.

Doi:10.1037/0022351475133

National Commission on Terrorist Attacks upon the United

States. (2004). *Outline of the 9/11 plot: Staff statement no. 16.*

Washington, DC: National Commission on Terrorist Attacks upon the United States. NATO Advanced Research Workshop on Prevention, Detection and Response to Nuclear and Radiological **Threat, Apikyan, S., Diamond, D., Way, R., & North Atlantic Treaty Organization. (2008).** *Prevention, detection, and response to nuclear and radiological threats.* Dordrecht, Germany:Springer.

Naughton, J. (2014). *From Gutenberg to Zuckerberg: Disruptive innovation in the age of the Internet.* London, England: Quercus.

Naval Health Research Center, Prusaczyk, W. K., Stuster, J. W., Goforth, H. W., Jr., Beckett, M. B., & Hodgdon, J. A. (1998). Survey of physically demanding tasks of U.S. Navy explosive ordnance disposal (EOD) personnel. *PsycEXTRA Dataset.* doi:10.1037/e527642009-001

Newell, B. R., & Shanks, D. R. (2014). Unconscious influences on decision-making: A critical review. *Behavioral and Brain Sciences, 37,* 1-19.doi:10.1017/s0140525x12003214

Neely, A., & Hii, J. (2014). The innovative capacity of firms. *Nang Yan Business Journal, 1.* doi:10.2478/nybj-2014-0007

Noble, K. A. (1998). *Classic quotes: 500 BC-AD 500; Aesop to Plato to Sappho to Zeno].* Friedrichsdorf, Germany: English Press International.

202

Nolte, J. (2007). Homeostasis, motivation, and emotion. *Elsevier's Integrated Neuroscience*,185–199. doi:10.1016/b978-0-323-03409-8.50024-5

Nunes, I., Miles, S., Luck, M., Barbosa, S., & Lucena, C. (2015). Decision-making with natural language based preferences and psychology-inspired heuristics. *Engineering Applications of Artificial Intelligence*, *42*, 16–35. doi:10.1016/j.engappai.2015.03.008

O'Connor, K., Hallam, R., & Rachman, S. (1985). Fearlessness and courage: A Replication experiment. *British Journal of Psychology*, *76*(2), 187. doi: 10.1111/j.2044-8295.1985.tb01942.x

Ordóñez, L. D., Benson, L., & Pittarello, A. (2015). Time-pressure perception and decision-Making. *The Wiley Blackwell Handbook of Judgment and Decision Making*, 517-542 doi:10.1002/9781118468333.ch18

Overton, l., Craig, I., & Perkins, R., (2016, February). *The impact of explosive weapons 2011-14.* Retrieved from http://reliefweb.int/sites/reliefweb.int/files/resources/Wide-Area Impact-explosive-weapons-in-populated-areas.pdf

Pelé, M., & Sueur, C. (2013). Decision-making theories: Linking the disparate research areas of individual and collective cognition. *Animal Cognition, 16*, 543-556. doi:10.1007/s10071-013-0631-1

Petri, H. L., & Govern, J. M. (2013). *Motivation: Theory, research, and application.* Belmont, CA: Wadsworth, Cengage Learning.

Pfister, H., & Böhm, G. (2014). Independent decisions are fictional from a psychological perspective. *Behavioral and Brain Sciences, 37*(1), 95-96. doi:10.1017/s0140525x13001830

Pisanu, F., & Menapace, P. (2014). Creativity & innovation: Four key issues from a literature review. *Creative Education, 5*, 145–154. doi:10.4236/ce.2014.53023

Pink, D. H. (2009). *Drive: The surprising truth about what motivates us.* New York, NY: Riverhead Books.

Pittman, T. (1987). Social motivation. *Annual Review of Psychology, 38*, 461–489. doi:10.1146/annurev.psych.38.1.461

Plattner, H., & Leukert, B. (2015). Rethink to innovate. *The In-Memory Revolution,* 1–11. doi:10.1007/978-3-319-16673-5_1

Polkinghorne, D. E. (1989). Phenomenological research methods. *Existential-Phenomenological Perspectives in Psychology,* 41–60. doi:10.1007/978-1-4615-6989-3_3

Revill, J. (2016). *Improvised explosive devices: The paradigmatic weapon of new wars.* New York, NY: Palgrave MacMillan.

Ritala, P., & Hurmelinna-Laukkanen, P. (2012). Incremental and radical innovation in coopetition-the role of absorptive capacity and appropriability. *Journal of Production Innovation Management, 30,* 154–169. doi:10.1111/j.1540-5885.2012.00956.x

Robb, J. (2007). *Brave new war: The next stage of terrorism and the end of globalization.*Hoboken, NJ: Wiley & Sons.

Rolls, E. T. (2007). Reward- and punishment-related learning; emotion and motivation.*Memory, Attention, and Decision-Making,* 113–261. doi:10.1093/acprof:oso/9780199232703.003.0003

Rosenthal, U., & Pijnenburg, B. (Eds.). (1991). *Crisis management and decision-making.* doi:10.1007/978-94-011-3398-2

Rossberger, R. J. (2014). National personality profiles and innovation: The role of cultural practices. *Creativity and Innovation Management, 23,* 331–348. doi:10.1111/caim.12075

Samli, A. C. (2011). Thinking outside of the box. *From Imagination to Innovation, 3,* 31–34.

doi:10.1007/978-1-4614-0854-3_5

Sawyer, R. K. (2013). *Explaining creativity: The science of human innovation.* Oxford, England: Oxford University Press.

Sawyer, K., & Bunderson, S. (2013). Innovation: A Review of Research in Organizational Behavior. Innovation and Growth, 13–55. doi:10.1142/9789814343558_0002

Schumpeter, J. A. (1911). *The theory of economic development.* New York, NY: Oxford University.

Schwarzer, R. (1992). *Self-efficacy: Thought control of action.* New York, NY: Taylor & Francis. doi:10.4324/9781315800820

Scribner, D. R. (2015). Predictors of shoot-don't shoot decision-making performance: An examination of cognitive and emotional factors. *Journal of Cognitive Engineering and Decision-Making, 10,* 3–13. doi:10.1177/1555343415608974

Sciullo, N., Walklate, S., & Mythen, G. (2015), Contradictions of terrorism: Security,risk and resilience. *Journal of Terrorism Research, 6.* doi:10.15664/jtr.1158

Self, D. R., Henry, E. D. V., Findley, C. S., & Reilly, E. (2007). Thrill seeking: The type T personality and extreme sports. *International Journal of Sport Management and Marketing, 2*(1/2), 175. doi:10.1504/ijsmm.2007.011397

Seligman, M., & Csikszentmihalyi, M. (2000). Positive

psychology: An introduction. *American Psychologist*, 55(1), 5–14.

doi:10.1037/0003-066x.55.1.5

Smelser, N. J., & Baltes, P. B. (2001). Editors-in-Chief.

International Encyclopedia of the Social & Behavioral Sciences, 3.

doi:10.1016/b0-08-043076-7/04694-5

Smith, G. R. (1997). *Demo men: Harrowing true stories from the*

military's elite bomb squads. New York, NY: Pocket Books.

Smith, J. A., Flowers, P., & Larkin, M. (2009). *Interpretative*

phenomenological analysis: Theory, method, and research. Los

Angeles, CA: Sage.

Smith, J. A. (2011A). Evaluating the contribution of interpretative

phenomenological analysis. *Health Psychology Review, 5*, 9-27.

doi: 10.1080/17437199.2010.510659

Smith, J. A. (2011B). Evaluating the contribution of interpretative

phenomenological analysis: Reply to the commentaries and further

development of criteria. *Health Psychology Review, 5,* 55-61. doi:

10.1080/17437199.2010.541743

Sousa, D. (2014). Validation in qualitative research: General aspects

and specificities of the descriptive phenomenological method.

Qualitative Research in Psychology, 11, 211–227.

doi:10.1080/14780887.2013.853855

Stagner, R. (1977). Homeostasis, discrepancy, dissonance. *Motive and Emotion, 1*(2), 103–138. doi:10.1007/bf00998515

Styles, G., & Perrin, R. (1975). *Bombs have no pity: My war against terrorism.* London, UK: Luscombe.

Suckley, L. (2015). Work and occupational psychology: Integrating theory and practice. *The International Journal of Entrepreneurship and Innovation, 16*, 228–228. doi:10.5367/ijei.2015.0194

Sun, B., & Zeng, Z. (2014). Proactive personality and job performance. *Management Innovation and Information Technology.* doi:10.2495/miit132282

Thackray, A., & Brock, D. C. (2015). *Moore's law: The life of Gordon Moore, Silicon Valley's quiet revolutionary.* New York, NY: Basic Books.

Thurman, J. (2011). Practical bomb scene investigation (2nd ed.). *Practical Aspects of Criminal & Forensic Investigations.* doi:10.1201/b10713

Tversky, A., & Kahneman D. (1973). Availability: A heuristic for judging frequency and probability. *Cognitive Psychology, 5*, 207

232. doi: 10.1016/0100-0285(73)90033-9

Tversky, A., & Kahneman, D. (1974). Judgment under uncertainty: Heuristics and biases. *Science*, 185, 1124–1131. doi: 10.1126/science.185.41.57.1124

Tversky, A., & Kahneman, D. (1982). Judgment of and by representativeness. In D. Kahneman, P. Slovic, & A. Tversky (Eds.), *Judgment under uncertainty: Heuristics and biases* (pp. 84–100). New York, NY: Cambridge University Press.

Tversky, A., & Kahneman, D. (1983). Extensional versus intuitive reasoning: The conjunction fallacy in probability judgment. *Psychological Review*, 90, 293–315.

Ullén, F., Hambrick, D. Z., & Mosing, M. A. (2016). Rethinking expertise: A multifactorial gene–environment interaction model of expert performance. *Psychological Bulletin*, 142, 427-446. doi:10.1037/bul0000033

U. S. Army Pacific (July, 2016). Asia-Pacific IED trends. Retrieved from www.usarpac.army.mil

U. S. Navy Explosive Ordnance Disposal Association. (1992).

History of U.S. navy bomb disposal. Virginia Beach, VA: Navy

Explosive Ordnance Disposal Association

U.S. Navy. (2016). *Explosive ordnance disposal (EOD) technician.*

Retrieved from http://navy.com/careers/special-

operations/eod.html#ft-key-responsibilities

U. S. Pacific Command (March, 2016). *USPACOM area of*

responsibility. http://www.pacom.mil/About-USPACOM

von Bertalanffy, L. (1969). *General system theory: Foundations,*

development, applications. New York, NY: George Braziller.

von Hippel, E. (2013). User innovation. *Leading Open Innovation,*

117–138. doi:10.7551/mitpress/9780262018494.003.0155

Wagstaff, C. D., & Leach, J. (2015). The value of strength-based

approaches in SERE and sport psychology. *Military Psychology,*

27(2), 65-84. doi:10.1037/mil0000066

Weiss, L., Whitaker, E., Briscoe, E., & Trewhitt, E. (2011).

Evaluating counter-IED strategies. *Defense & Security Analysis, 27,*

135–147. doi:10.1080/14751798.2011.578717

Wiggins, O. P., & Schwartz, M. A. (2015). Phenomenological

concept of intentionality. *The Encyclopedia of Clinical Psychology*,

1–4. doi:10.1002/9781118625392.wbecp387

Wilder, W. D., Csikszentmihalyi, M., & Csikszentmihalyi, I. S.

(1989). Optimal experience: Psychological studies of flow in

consciousness. *Man, 24*, 690. doi:10.2307/2804304

West, M. A., & Anderson, N. R. (1996). Innovation in top

management teams. *Journal of Applied Psychology, 81*, 680-693.

doi:10.1037/0021-9010.81.6.680

Wittes, B., & Blum, G. (2015). *The future of violence: Robots and

germs, hackers, and drones: Confronting a new age of threat.* New

York, NY: Basic Books.

Zestcott, C. A., Lifshin, U., Helm, P., & Greenberg, J. (2016). He

dies, he scores: Evidence that reminders of death motivate improved

performance in basketball. *Journal of Sport and Exercise

Psychology*, 1–40. doi:10.1123/jsep.2016-0025

Made in the USA
San Bernardino, CA
15 September 2017